Palgrave Studies in European Union Politics

Edited by: **Michelle Egan**, American University, USA, **Neill Nugent**, Visiting Professor, College of Europe, Bruges and Honorary Professor, University of Salford, UK, and **William Paterson OBE**, University of Aston, UK

Editorial Board: **Christopher Hill**, Cambridge, UK, **Simon Hix**, London School of Economics, UK, **Mark Pollack**, Temple University, USA, **Kalypso Nicolaïdis**, Oxford, UK, **Morten Egeberg**, University of Oslo, Norway, **Amy Verdun**, University of Victoria, Canada, **Claudio M. Radaelli**, University of Exeter, UK, **Frank Schimmelfennig**, Swiss Federal Institute of Technology, Switzerland

Following on the sustained success of the acclaimed *European Union Series*, which essentially publishes research-based textbooks, *Palgrave Studies in European Union Politics* publishes cutting-edge, research-driven monographs.

The remit of the series is broadly defined, both in terms of subject and academic discipline. All topics of significance concerning the nature and operation of the European Union potentially fall within the scope of the series. The series is multidisciplinary to reflect the growing importance of the EU as a political, economic and social phenomenon.

Titles include:

Carolyn Ban
MANAGEMENT AND CULTURE IN AN ENLARGED EUROPEAN COMMISSION
From Diversity to Unity?

Gijs Jan Brandsma
CONTROLLING COMITOLOGY
Accountability in a Multi-Level System

Renaud Dehousse (*editor*)
THE 'COMMUNITY METHOD'
Obstinate or Obsolete?

Kenneth Dyson and Angelos Sepos (*editors*)
WHICH EUROPE?
The Politics of Differentiated Integration

Michelle Egan, Neill Nugent, and William E. Paterson (*editors*)
RESEARCH AGENDAS IN EU STUDIES
Stalking the Elephant

Theofanis Exadaktylos and Claudio M. Radaelli (*editors*)
RESEARCH DESIGN IN EUROPEAN STUDIES
Establishing Causality in Europeanization

Jack Hayward and Rüdiger Wurzel (*editors*)
EUROPEAN DISUNION
Between Sovereignty and Solidarity

Wolfram Kaiser and Jan-Henrik Meyer (*editors*)
SOCIETAL ACTORS IN EUROPEAN INTEGRATION

Christian Kaunert and Sarah Leonard (*editors*)
EUROPEAN SECURITY, TERRORISM AND INTELLIGENCE
Tackling New Security Challenges in Europe

Christian Kaunert and Kamil Zwolski
The EU AS A GLOBAL SECURITY ACTOR
A Comprehensive Analysis Beyond CFSP and JHA

Marina Kolb
THE EUROPEAN UNION AND THE COUNCIL OF EUROPE

Finn Laursen (*editor*)

DESIGNING THE EUROPEAN UNION
From Paris to Lisbon

Karl-Oskar Lindgren and Thomas Persson
PARTICIPATORY GOVERNANCE IN THE EU
Enhancing or Endangering Democracy and Efficiency?

Daniel Naurin and Helen Wallace (*editors*)
UNVEILING THE COUNCIL OF THE EUROPEAN UNION
Games Governments Play in Brussels

Dimitris Papadimitriou and Paul Copeland (*editors*)
THE EU's LISBON STRATEGY
Evaluating Success, Understanding Failure

Emmanuelle Schon-Quinlivan
REFORMING THE EUROPEAN COMMISSION

Roger Scully and Richard Wyn Jones (*editors*)
EUROPE, REGIONS AND EUROPEAN REGIONALISM

Yves Tiberghien (*editor*)
LEADERSHIP IN GLOBAL INSTITUTION BUILDING
Minerva's Rule

Asle Toje
AFTER THE POST-COLD WAR
The European Union as a Small Power

Liubomir K. Topaloff
POLITICAL PARTIES AND EUROSCEPTICISM

Richard G. Whitman and Stefan Wolff (*editors*)
THE EUROPEAN NEIGHBOURHOOD POLICY IN PERSPECTIVE
Context, Implementation and Impact

Richard G. Whitman (*editor*)
NORMATIVE POWER EUROPE
Empirical and Theoretical Perspectives

Sarah Wolff
THE MEDITERRANEAN DIMENSION OF THE EUROPEAN UNION'S INTERNAL SECURITY

Jan Wouters, Hans Bruyninckx, Sudeshna Basu and Simon Schunz (*editors*)
THE EUROPEAN UNION AND MULTILATERAL GOVERNANCE
Assessing EU Participation in United Nations Human Rights and Environmental Fora

---

Palgrave Studies in European Union Politics
Series Standing Order ISBN 978–1–403–99511–7 (hardback) and
ISBN 978–1–403–99512–4 (paperback)

You can receive future titles in this series as they are published by placing a standing order. Please contact your bookseller or, in case of difficulty, write to us at the address below with your name and address, the title of the series and one of the ISBNs quoted above.

Customer Services Department, Macmillan Distribution Ltd, Houndmills, Basingstoke, Hampshire RG21 6XS, UK.

Controlling Comitology
Accountability in a Multi-Level System

Gijs Jan Brandsma
Assistant Professor, Utrecht School of Governance, University of Utrecht

© Gijs Jan Brandsma 2013

All rights reserved. No reproduction, copy or transmission of this publication may be made without written permission.

No portion of this publication may be reproduced, copied or transmitted save with written permission or in accordance with the provisions of the Copyright, Designs and Patents Act 1988, or under the terms of any licence permitting limited copying issued by the Copyright Licensing Agency, Saffron House, 6–10 Kirby Street, London EC1N 8TS.

Any person who does any unauthorized act in relation to this publication may be liable to criminal prosecution and civil claims for damages.

The author has asserted his right to be identified as the author of this work in accordance with the Copyright, Designs and Patents Act 1988.

First published 2013 by
PALGRAVE MACMILLAN

Palgrave Macmillan in the UK is an imprint of Macmillan Publishers Limited, registered in England, company number 785998, of Houndmills, Basingstoke, Hampshire RG21 6XS.

Palgrave Macmillan in the US is a division of St Martin's Press LLC, 175 Fifth Avenue, New York, NY 10010.

Palgrave Macmillan is the global academic imprint of the above companies and has companies and representatives throughout the world.

Palgrave® and Macmillan® are registered trademarks in the United States, the United Kingdom, Europe and other countries.

ISBN 978–1–137–31963–0

This book is printed on paper suitable for recycling and made from fully managed and sustained forest sources. Logging, pulping and manufacturing processes are expected to conform to the environmental regulations of the country of origin.

A catalogue record for this book is available from the British Library.

A catalog record for this book is available from the Library of Congress.

Typeset by MPS Limited, Chennai, India.

Contents

List of Figures, Tables and Boxes	vi
Preface and Acknowledgements	viii
1 Hidden Power	1
2 Comitology: The System, the Committees and Their Participants	18
3 Accountability and Multi-Level Governance	44
4 System-Level Accountability: Conflict Over Control	63
5 Committee-Level Accountability: System Meets Practice	93
6 Participant-Level Accountability: Substantive Talks and Deafening Silence	119
7 Comitology and Multi-Level Accountability	145
Annex: Overview of Sources Regarding the Post-Lisbon Negotiations on Comitology	165
Notes	167
Bibliography	171
Index	183

List of Figures, Tables and Boxes

Figures

1.1	Acts adopted by the three institutions	3
1.2	Ratio between acts adopted by the three institutions	4
3.1	Multi-level accountability	59
4.1	Accountability in the pre-Maastricht comitology system	69
4.2	Accountability in the 1999/2006 comitology system	73
4.3	Accountability in the post-Lisbon comitology system	90
5.1	Information flow from comitology committee to MEP	109
6.1	A three-dimensional accountability assessment tool	139
6.2	The accountability cube	140
7.1	Multi-level accountability	148
7.2	Comitology's multi-level accountability from a popular control perspective	154
7.3	Comitology's multi-level accountability from a checks and balances perspective	159

Tables

2.1	Regulations, directives and decisions adopted by the European institutions between 2005 and 2011	22
2.2	Number of Commission acts passing through comitology	23
2.3	Number of comitology committees	28
2.4	Committees per Commission DG in 2011	34
2.5	Committee activity per Commission DG in 2011	35
4.1	Committee powers defined in the 1987 Comitology Decision	67
4.2	Committee powers defined in the 1999 and 2006 Comitology Decisions	72
4.3	Committee powers in the post-Lisbon comitology system	89

5.1	Interaction modes within comitology committees	99
5.2	Correlations between modes of interaction within comitology	100
5.3	Overview of the European Parliament's information rights for comitology	105
6.1	Style of representation	124
6.2	Information received by hierarchical superiors	128
6.3	Intensity of discussions	133
7.1	Three levels, two perspectives	160

Boxes

1.1	Thousands of little decisions	2
2.1	Comitology in practice	18
2.2	Excerpt from the Patients' Rights Directive (2011/24/EU)	28
2.3	Balancing national and European interests	40

Preface and Acknowledgements

This book is the result of many years of research into delegated decision-making in the European Union. While my earlier publications focused on either the workings of comitology more generally or on the accountability of national committee participants, the remit of this book is more extensive.

Surprisingly, empirical studies of EU accountability, or the workings of comitology, tend to focus on either European actors or national actors, but not on both. Hence, existing research, including my own contributions, presents only part of the picture. Only one level – rather than all those involved in policymaking – is taken into account. By contrast, this book explores accountability in truly multi-level terms, and aims to present the full picture.

I am indebted to Mark Bovens, Deirdre Curtin, Albert Meijer and Paul 't Hart who, in the year 2005, recruited me as a researcher for a broad-ranging project on EU accountability, funded by the Dutch science foundation NWO. They encouraged me to continue doing empirical research into normatively salient issues, particularly within the domain of European governance. Again, thanks go to Deirdre Curtin for enabling me to finish this manuscript as part of a broader research project, funded by a personal NWO *Spinoza* grant awarded to her.

Further thanks go to Jens Blom-Hansen, Arjen Boin, Sanneke Kuipers, Huib Pellikaan, Sietse Ringers, Rinus van Schendelen, Thomas Schillemans, Marianne van de Steeg, Harmen van der Veer, Liesa Veldman and many others for their excellent cooperation, helpful suggestions and stimulating discussions. I also thank the many respondents in Brussels, Copenhagen and The Hague, without whom it would not have been possible to conduct this research.

Special thanks go to the late Peter Mair, who allowed me to dedicate myself to preparing the typescript during two months at the EUI in Florence. I also thank all colleagues at the EUI for fruitful and inspiring discussions on comitology as well as on the state of the European Union more generally.

Some of the material presented in Chapter 6 appeared in *The Real World of EU Accountability* (edited by Mark Bovens, Deirdre Curtin and Paul 't Hart). I am grateful to Oxford University Press for allowing me to reuse this material here. And finally, although Herman was pleased that he was not expected to serve as my first critic, I am positive that this volume greatly benefited from his presence.

1
Hidden Power

Introduction

Each day, thousands of national civil servants travel to Brussels from all over the European Union: sometimes for consultation, such as when the European Commission asks for expert advice before sending a legislative proposal to the Council of Ministers and to the European Parliament (EP) (Larsson, 2003a); and at other times to work out agreements amongst each other before the Council legislates (Fouilleux et al., 2005) or to deal with executive measures drafted by the Commission (Blom-Hansen, 2011a, 2011b).

When speaking of the European Union, its institutions immediately spring to mind. The European Commission, the European Parliament, the Council of Ministers and the Courts are all well-known actors; they are in the spotlight of the European Union, so to speak. What goes unseen, however, is how deeply involved backstage actors are in the decision-making processes. Although operating on the political sidelines, these hidden actors have a marked impact on the majority of Union decisions, including those concerning very salient political matters.

Backstage Europe is the realm of committees. Van Alphen (Box 1.1) is the official representative of the Netherlands in one of the committees that advises on executive measures drafted by the Commission. This type of committee is part of what is known as 'comitology' in EU jargon, and most such committees meet in Centre Borschette, a nondescript conference centre in Rue Froissart, Brussels. All member states participate in comitology committees by sending one or two of their civil servants. The comitology system is specifically designed to advise the Commission on the content of these executive measures: norms, standards, funding schemes and so on. It is a powerful form of advice: in the comitology system, measures proposed by the Commission must first either be voted on by the committee members or they may be vetoed by the Council or the European Parliament on the basis of the committees' advice. Comitology is a huge system. It is composed of some 220 committees, which discuss and vote on up to half of all European decisions, directives and regulations.[1] In this respect, the system produces far more acts than the Council and the European Parliament do legislation.

Box 1.1   Thousands of little decisions

> Corné Van Alphen (aged 39) traveled from The Hague to Brussels this morning on an early train. He works as rural development policy advisor for the Dutch Ministry of Agriculture. He cordially greets his colleagues from other countries; most are also policy advisors working for agriculture ministries. Here at Borschette, Europe appears to be run by grade 13 civil servants (intermediate level).
> [...]
> All proposals are accepted unanimously. Scandinavian farmers can start working with their high-tech ovens. Their colleagues elsewhere in Europe will be paid for maintaining hedges and wooded banks. The civil servants who voted on this leave for lunch.
> [...]
> Do civil servants like Van Alphen have a lot of power when they are in Borschette? 'No', he says. [...] 'But come to think of it', Van Alphen ponders while prodding his pasta, 'when you add up all these thousands of decisions that we make across the road in Borschette, which often have a very practical influence, in this case on the future of farmers, well, then it is quite a powerful institution'.
>
> *Source*: NRC Handelsblad, 'Een olievlek van ambtenaren', 14 May 2005.

Backstage Europe and executive rule-making

Massive numbers of little rules

Even though many scholars focus on the legislative practices of the European institutions, the vast majority of European decisions, directives and regulations are, in actual fact, of an executive nature (Van Schendelen, 2010, p. 69–71). Obviously, the aims and principles of policy are embodied in legislation that is adopted by the Council of Ministers and the European Parliament, mostly according to the well-known co-decision or ordinary legislative procedure. But most legislation does not specify in detail who is affected by it and by what means. That is considered to be a matter for the executive. The executive produces a much greater number of 'little rules' that come in the form of decisions, directives and regulations and are adopted by the Commission. In short, the legislative acts specify the principles, while the Commission's executive measures flesh these out into tangible measures, linking these broad policy objectives to specific citizens, companies, regions or states.

Figures 1.1 and 1.2 are instructive for understanding how many decisions are made in the executive sphere. Figure 1.1 shows the absolute number of decisions, directives and regulations that have been adopted by the three institutions since 1971. In Figure 1.2, the share of each of the institutions in the total is displayed for the same period. Although the legislative co-decision acts receive most attention by far, they only constitute a tiny fraction of the total. Throughout history, the vast majority of European directives, decisions and regulations have been executive acts adopted by the Commission.

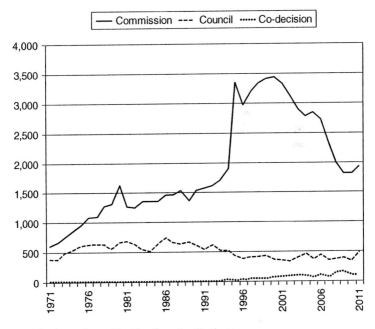

Figure 1.1 Acts adopted by the three institutions

Source: EUR-LEX, http://eur-lex.europa.eu, including all Decisions, Directives and Regulations, irrespective of Treaty base, adopted exclusively by the Commission or the Council, or under the co-decision procedure.

4 *Controlling Comitology*

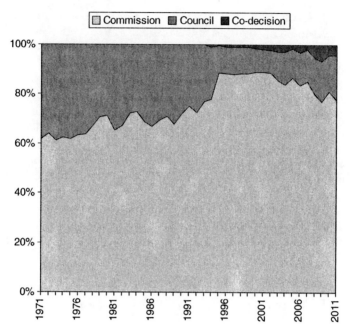

Figure 1.2 Ratio between acts adopted by the three institutions
Source: EUR-LEX, http://eur-lex.europa.eu, including all Decisions, Directives and Regulations, irrespective of Treaty base, adopted exclusively by the Commission or the Council, or under the co-decision procedure.

This is also where the executive's chief backstage actor comes into the picture. Comitology is deeply involved in crafting and negotiating these little rules, and in deciding on who gets what, how and when. Between 45 and 60 per cent of the Commission's acts first have to pass a comitology committee before they can be adopted. In terms of volume, this makes comitology the most important governance process of the European Union. Next to executive decisions, directives and regulations, the Commission also adopts 'working programmes', 'action programmes', funding allocations and many more executive measures that are also subject to deliberation in the comitology committees but which do not make it into the Official Journal. In total, the committees have voted between 2,000 and 2,500 times per year over the past decade, which allowed the Commission to adopt about the same number of executive measures, in addition to a smaller number of measures for which no committee opinion was required.[2] Hence executive decision-making in the European Union is an important, highly intricate affair, involving a myriad of backstage actors who effectively set their stamp on the majority of all Union acts.

Let's run through a few examples to show how comitology decision-making relates to political decision-making and how it affects the lives of European citizens. In the Habitats Directive, for example (Council Directive 92/43/EEC), the Council expressed its political will to protect certain species and environmental sites, and established the mechanism that any damage occurring to these must be compensated. But the decisions on which specific species and areas to protect were delegated to the executive, assisted by a comitology committee of national civil service experts in the field of environmental protection. The same can be said with respect to decisions regarding airlines to be put on a black list, the size of tomatoes, safety measures at work, technical standards for trains and railway lines, the safety of toys and many more examples.

Some of these issues may appear to be rather technical, perhaps even boring. But there are plenty of examples where technical matters can be politically quite salient matters. Standards for animal health and animal disease control, for instance, were considered to be political non-issues in the early 1990s, but since the outbreak of BSE they have turned into politically contested issues (Harlow, 2002, p. 70–1). Whether or not specific genetically modified organisms can be released into the environment is also both a technical and a political discussion. These are only a handful of examples out of the thousands of little decisions that together make comitology powerful. Although these particular issues bear much political salience, this is not typical for the bulk of committee activity. Nonetheless, even politically non-salient issues are important. After all, all decision-making comes with winners and losers. To those who are directly affected by new legislation, the devil is usually not in the objectives of legislation but rather in the detail of implementation (Van Schendelen and Scully, 2006, 6).

The power of comitology

Given the technical nature of the issues comitology deals with, it is not surprising that expertise is needed for effective participation. Hence, participants in comitology are usually policy specialists working in national ministries or agencies, who, once in Brussels, take on the role of member state representative. For them, membership of a comitology committee is an international extension of their day-to-day work 'at home' (Egeberg, Schäfer and Trondal, 2003, 21–2).

The power of comitology is vested not only in the expertise of its participants but also in the formal position of the comitology committees in the Commission's processes of adopting executive measures. There are two different modes by which the committee members affect Union policies, which are only briefly discussed at this point but which are looked at more extensively in Chapters 2 and 4. The first mode is based on Article 291 of the Treaty on the Functioning of the European Union (hereafter referred to as TFEU), which provides that mechanisms must be put in place by which the member states can control the Commission's exercise of its implementing powers. These mechanisms of control are further specified in a Council and Parliament Regulation (2011/182/EU), hereafter referred to as the 2011 Comitology Regulation. Under this regulation, the Commission must present drafts of implementing measures to committees of member state representatives, who are empowered to block their adoption. Depending on the voting procedure used in the committee and the results of the vote, the Commission can either adopt its proposed measure, resubmit an amended version of the same measure to the same committee, decide not to adopt the measure at all, or it can forward the original measure that was blocked by the committee to an appeal body (which, before the entry into force of the Lisbon Treaty, was the Council of Ministers) (see Council Decision 1999/468/EC, Council and Parliament Regulation 2011/182/EU). Apart from the binding effects of the outcomes of such votes, there is another reason why the Commission needs to secure support from the committees. Since most, if not all, European executive measures are required to be further implemented at the national level, the member states send the same policy specialists to the committee meetings who are assigned to implement those policies at the national level. In practice, therefore, the Commission cannot adopt executive measures swiftly without the formal approval of a comitology committee, let alone ones that are seen as effective. For this reason, the Commission works hard to secure a positive vote in the committees, as testified by the fact that often the same issues are repeatedly put on the committees' agenda, and by the very low number of negative votes or referrals to the appeal body (Alfé et al., 2009, p. 145).

The second mode is based on Article 290 (TFEU), which applies in cases of 'delegated legislation'. In such cases, a legislative act grants the Commission the power to supplement or amend 'non-essential elements' of existing Council and Parliamentary legislation. This refers, for instance, to amending certain elements in an act's technical annexes (for example, lists of dangerous substances in directives on safety, lists of endangered species in directives on environmental protection, et cetera). In the very final stages of drafting a piece of delegated legislation, the

Commission consults a committee of 'experts', which in practice represent the member states.³ The Commission subsequently forwards this draft – together with the committee opinion – to the Council of Ministers and the European Parliament, both of which are also kept informed of all committee proceedings. Once the delegated act is finalized and forwarded, both the Council and the Parliament may oppose it and thereby block its adoption, or even revoke the delegation of legislative powers to the Commission completely (Article 290 TFEU, European Parliament, Council of Ministers and European Commission, 2011). Since the implementation of the Lisbon Treaty, in a formal sense these committees have become part of the Commission's expert group system (see Chapter 4), which is why, in a very strict legal sense, they are no longer part of comitology, even though their members are made up of the same people and the committees may still vote – albeit not with binding effect (European Commission, 2010a, 15).

The fact that the system currently consists of two modes is the result of a protracted inter-institutional battle between the European Parliament and the Council of Ministers. Historically, the European Parliament had very little influence on the functioning of the comitology system; however, with the entry into effect of the Lisbon Treaty, a delegated legislation regime with extensive control rights for the European Parliament and no formal role for committees was introduced. This led some commentators to argue that in the new situation, reference should be made to delegated and implementing acts rather than comitology (for example, Peers and Costa, 2012). Others continue to speak of comitology, while taking into account the differences between the two newly introduced regimes (for example, Hardacre and Kaeding, 2011; Héritier et al., 2012, p. 134). Because the origins of the two systems are related, because both operate as mechanisms for controlling the European Commission's activities and because both systems include committees of member state representatives, this book embraces the latter view, referring to these two together systems when speaking of comitology or of committee members. Obviously, however, the fundamental differences between the two systems are detailed throughout this book.

Comitology, accountability and democracy

The irony of accountability

Formally speaking, comitology participants act as delegates of the national administrations. They would therefore be expected to bargain with the other member states' representatives and the Commission in order to favour their own national interest as much as possible. However, much of the available evidence suggests that there are many cases in which committee meetings are not characterized by intense negotiations but rather by a more deliberative form of interaction. This phenomenon, termed 'supranational deliberation' (Joerges and Neyer, 1997a), implies that committee members tend primarily to search for the common good from a professional point of view (see Joerges and Neyer, 1997a; Pollack, 2003a). In the eyes of many participants, finding the best *technical* solution would appear to be more important than advancing their own national interests. The meetings are characterized by a spirit of expertise, scientific evidence plays a prominent role, and formal power seems to be of minor interest (Wessels, 1998, 225; Sannerstedt, 2005, p. 105).

No matter how sound the results produced by the comitology system may be (Joerges, 2006), concerns have been voiced as to the degree to which comitology is an accountable form of governance (Radaelli, 1999, 770–1; Schäfer, 2000, p. 22–3; Harlow, 2002, p. 67–71; Rhinard, 2002, 196–203; Van Schendelen, 2006, 37). Comitology is concerned with fleshing out the details of well over 2,000 measures per year. On the basis of its input, the Commission may decide to draft a measure in a particular way so that it can be sure of its acceptance once the matter is voted upon in a committee under Article 291 (TFEU) or after it is forwarded to the other institutions under Article 290 (TFEU). The number of times issues appear and re-appear on the agenda of committee meetings means either that the Commission anticipates what is acceptable to a majority of the committee, or that it is deliberating with the committee members in a consensual way, in order to find an optimal outcome together (Alfé et al., 2009, p. 145–6). In both interpretations, comitology effectively acts as decision-maker for a wide range of policy issues, and hence should also be able to be held accountable.[4]

Yet the irony of comitology is that it was designed to be a control device in itself. When the first common policies were to be implemented in the early 1960s, the member states in the Council feared that they would not be able to control the Commission when it exercised its executive powers. The comitology system was created as a means to mitigate this risk. By obliging the Commission to present its executive proposals to a comitology committee consisting of member state representatives, the Council aimed to keep the Commission in check for matters where it felt such special obligations were necessary (Bergström, 2005, p. 43–57; Blom-Hansen, 2008, 2011b, p. 53–71).

Increasingly, however, concern about the accountability of comitology has been voiced. Comitology involves a large number of civil servants, and the member states can send their people to the committees, whereas the European Parliament – as co-legislator to the Council – seems barely involved (Neuhold, 2001; Bradley, 2008). The meetings are only attended by the relevant specialists (Joerges and Neyer, 1997a) and are not held in public (Neuhold, 2001). Minutes – insofar as they can be traced on the Internet – are either uninformative or incomprehensible to outsiders (Brandsma et al., 2008). And, last but not least, comitology produces most of the detailed regulations, directives and decisions for which the European Union is renowned, including the recently repealed regulations on quality standards for bananas and cucumbers of different lengths and shapes.[5]

Comitology and the democratic deficit

Many of the reasons for which citizens tend to dislike European governance also seem to apply to comitology *en miniature*. This raises questions as to the democratic quality of comitology decision-making. Does the often-cited 'democratic deficit' of the European Union manifest itself in backstage Europe too? Even though there is no consensus on what the term 'democracy' actually means within the context of a supranational organization (Abromeit, 2007), let alone how 'deficits' can be detected and how they can be repaired, a rich body of literature has emerged on this topic that shows that this is a matter of perspective. The three most common approaches to the democratic deficit are respectively inspired by intergovernmentalism (the perspective of the member states, that is, the Council) supranationalism (the perspective of the supranational institutions, that is, the Commission, the Courts and the European Parliament) and the 'regulatory state'.

To begin with the latter, the 'regulatory state' perspective regards European governance as purely regulatory: member states keep the most salient policies to themselves or delegate them to independent regulators or agencies. According to this perspective, the European Union deals solely with depoliticized, non-distributive issues for which there is no need for common democratic standards other than transparency and accountability, as long as the supranational powers are clearly defined (Majone, 1998, 14–28). But this view ignores the fact that regulatory affairs, too, come with winners and losers and can, therefore, certainly be politicized (Follesdal and Hix, 2006, 542–4). The very existence of comitology would appear to be at odds with this perspective, as it shows that member states care about voicing their opinion in this seemingly apolitical domain (Joerges, 2006, 783–4).

Nor does either of the other two perspectives, that is, intergovernmentalism and supranationalism, fit comfortably with the system of comitology and other forms of governance in the European Union. Many recent studies of European Union governance show fusion processes between European and domestic administrative actors (for example, Wessels, 1997; Hofmann and Türk, 2007; Trondal, 2009). Innumerable actors at the national and even sub-national level collaborate with European actors in co-operative settings and work towards common positions. This is referred to as 'multi-level governance' (for example, Marks et al., 1996; Scharpf, 1997; Hooghe and Marks, 2003; Bache and Flinders, 2004). Both intergovernmentalism and supranationalism sit poorly with multi-level forms of governance, as they tend to focus on either the member states (with the Council as their agent) or (mainly) on the Commission. Effectively, these approaches are more geared to elucidating only one particular aspect in the multi-level complexity of many 'new' forms of European governance. Hence for an accurate depiction of European governance practices, the two logics must come together.

Comitology is a case in point of multi-level governance: although installed and staffed by the member states, its participants nonetheless have a tendency to search for technically sound solutions under the chairmanship of the Commission. Comitology is therefore not a purely intergovernmental system, nor is it a purely supranational system: it is a system in which both logics come together and in which the Commission and the member states are mutually dependent (Wessels, 1998).

This empirical evidence calls for a more sophisticated perspective on European democracy than either supranationalism or intergovernmentalism can deliver. According to a supranational approach, for example, citizen representation and accountability must be ensured in order for there to be valid decision-making at the European level (for example, Decker, 2002). The main issues for comitology at the European level from this perspective are to what extent representation of the European citizens is ensured and to what extent the activities of the committees are visible to the European Parliament. It is this line of thinking about democratic deficits to which studies on comitology's legitimacy relate most, as they are generally concerned with relationships between institutions and with the role of the European Parliament in particular (Schäfer, 1996, p. 22, 2000, p. 22–3; Larsson, 2003b, p. 169–71; Christiansen and Vaccari, 2006; Bradley, 2008; Neuhold, 2008; Christiansen and Dobbels, 2012). As comitology is an important governance tool in executive decision-making, the above-mentioned observations about the lack of public scrutiny and limited or unutilized opportunities for parliamentary involvement constitute a democratic legitimacy problem for comitology (see Chapter 2).

The intergovernmental perspective on democracy in the European Union, by contrast, directs attention away from arrangements between European institutions per se (for example, Moravcsik, 2002). Here, the democratic legitimacy of comitology must mainly be found in the links between citizens of member states, member state governments and the member state delegates attending comitology committees. From this perspective, the key question is to what extent comitology committee members express the will of their home governments and to what extent their home governments hold them to account for their input in the committees (Brandsma, 2010a).

The academic discourse on EU democracy, thus, tends to be mono-focused on either the European or the national level. Given the nature of multi-level governance settings such as comitology, however, a focus on one or the other is overly simplistic. Therefore, this book aims to give the full picture by addressing the accountability of comitology, taking both the European and the national level into account. It does so not only by looking at the formal procedures of comitology and tracing where and to what extent accountability mechanisms are present and where these are lacking, but also by exploring their actual functioning.

Accountability and multi-level governance

How accountable is comitology decision-making, *de jure* and *de facto*? This question is not only relevant to the study of comitology but also to other multi-level forms of governance in which individual or member state participation meets collective action. Independent national regulators in the telecommunications or energy markets, for instance, meet regularly in European networks, after which the Commission uses their advice in new regulations, if the national regulators have not yet voluntarily introduced such measures in their own states, as a result of informal coordination (Eberlein and Grande, 2005; Coen and Thatcher, 2008). Similar but more formalized processes can be seen in the working parties of the Council and COREPER, where member state representatives work towards a common Council position (Fouilleux et al., 2005; Häge, 2008).

Ensuring accountability in a multi-level organization is a challenge in its own right. The collective decisions that are made stem from bargaining processes: after all, in the end, the involved actors need to be able to defend the collective decision 'at home', while at the same time convincingly asserting that they have done their utmost to benefit their country's interest as much as possible. They play a 'two-level game', so to speak (Putnam, 1988). At the same time, the eventual decisions are made at a higher level of aggregation than the various 'lower' accountability forums can relate to. For example, comitology decisions are adopted by the European Commission and have a legally binding effect throughout the European Union. National accountability forums, such as parliaments or even national ministries, are simply not equipped to oversee the union-wide implications of such decisions. There, the European Parliament could almost naturally play a meaningful role (Curtin and Egeberg, 2008, 652), because it is a political actor at the supranational level, and it has a constitutional role to scrutinize the Commission. However, it is not in a position to control the activities of member state representatives in comitology committees – which is the very essence of the system.

From the above, it follows that the question of the accountability of multi-level governance settings is a salient one, both *de jure* and *de facto*. But empirical research into accountability is scarce, to say the least. Even though there is an extensive body of work on accountability, most studies are of a conceptual or game-theoretical nature. The game-theoretical studies of accountability generally make use of the 'principal-agent framework', which is also well known in the literature on delegation. This framework is used in descriptive accounts of political systems (such as Damgaard, 2000) and is further developed by means of formal models (for instance, Lupia, 2006). As will be argued in the next chapter, this is only one approach to analysing accountability. Constitutional lawyers have developed a tradition of analysing decision-making systems in terms of the checks and balances provided for in them, and the degree to which accountability is instrumental in providing for these checks and balances. In the literature on accountability, however, strong emphasis is placed on the definition of the term itself, including indication of different typologies and styles of accountability, discussions of its relevance for a democratic system and warnings with respect to the perils of some problematic aspects of the concept as such (Behn, 2001; Mulgan, 2003; Strøm, 2006; Bovens, 2007a; Black, 2008).

By taking an empirical approach, this study aims to augment our understanding of the workings of an accountability regime in a multi-level context. It therefore makes use of an empirical measurement of the concept, explicitly taking into account the multi-level nature of comitology decision-making. In this way, even though the study is limited to comitology, the outcomes will hopefully also serve as helpful suggestions for the study of accountability in a more general sense when applied to the actual behaviour of individuals and groups. As the above discussion indicated, accountability is an essential element from any perspective on democracy in the European Union. But apart from the fact that its relevance hardly seems contested, only little is known about the actual workings of accountability in the European Union (Bovens et al., 2010).

Comitology: The system, the committees and its participants

In order to fully capture the accountability of comitology decision-making, three levels of analysis are used throughout this book: the *system level*, the *committee level* and the *participants' level*.

The *system level* refers to the constitutional setup of comitology. It addresses which entities or institutions delegate powers to each other, what the powers of each of the involved actors are and what forms of accountability are provided for in the formal structure of comitology. In this respect, several structural accountability flaws can be detected, most notably concerning the powers of the European Parliament but also regarding the Council of Ministers. The system level, thus, covers the *de jure* aspect of comitology accountability.

The *committee level* addresses the *de facto* accountability of the individual committees that together make up the comitology system towards forums at the European level. Of all institutions, the European Parliament has the most pronounced role in this, despite its lack of powers in parts of the comitology system. Using information on comitology committees that it either receives directly from the Commission or from stakeholders in the field, it selectively looks into matters it considers important and occasionally takes action. Relevant issues at the committee level include the quality and timing of information, preparatory work that is done by European Parliament staff, interest of MEPs in comitology matters and consequences that the European Parliament in practice imposes.

The final level of analysis is the *participant's level*, which includes the *de facto* accountability of the member state civil servants participating in comitology vis-à-vis their superiors in their home organizations. The relevant issues at this level are the same as at the committee level, only in this case applying to single participants.

As will be argued further on in greater detail, all three levels of accountability are complementary and essential for the accountability of multi-level governance settings. In the end, the power of member state representatives lies in the input they provide and, where applicable, in their vote. It makes no sense for them to be accountable to a

European-level actor since they represent their own member states only. Simultaneously, the acts that pass through the comitology system are European acts adopted by the Commission, which necessitates accountability towards the European legislative institutions. Accountability arrangements are required across the system as a whole that enable a democratic accountability of comitology, by both European and national actors. Moreover, in practice, both types of actors need to adjust their behaviour and priorities in order to be able to hold comitology decision-making as a whole accountable.

The organization of this book

Including this introduction, this study is organized into seven chapters. For the benefit of those readers who are not familiar with the system of comitology and its function in European policy making, Chapter 2 describes this system in more detail. It does so according to the three levels that were introduced above: the *system* of comitology, the *committees* that together make up the comitology system and the *participants within the committees*. First, the chapter discusses the *system* level of comitology by giving a brief introduction of what comitology is, depicting its function in the policy process and showing how the Council, the Commission and the European Parliament are involved in comitology. This part also demonstrates in greater detail the fact that comitology is the main executive governance process in the European Union in terms of the volume of acts passing through it. Next, the chapter focuses on the *committees* that together make up the comitology system. What exactly makes a committee, and how many are there? What kind of policies do the committees handle, and how much activity do they display? As will appear in this section, official definitions of what comitology committees constitute differ significantly from what functions as a committee in actual practice, and likewise, what the committees deal with in practice. The third section examines the committee members. Who do the member states send to the comitology committee meetings, and in what way do they try to reach agreements? Again, this section shows that practices often differ significantly as to what might be expected on the basis of the constitutional setup of the system. For each respective level, the chapter specifically addresses the most important aspects of accountability on each of these levels, which are then further analysed in following chapters.

Chapter 3 presents an operational definition of accountability and works towards a framework for analysing *de jure* and *de facto* accountability in a multi-level context. It argues that existing perspectives on accountability are mono-focused on either inter-institutional relationships at the European level or on practices at the national level, while both are equally important to the functioning of the system. It shows that the presence of different layers of government leads many to expect this to be an obstacle to the accountability of collective decision-making arrangements, but that it is also at odds with many traditional conceptions of analysing accountability as such. This chapter argues that only an evaluation of accountability across all these layers will provide meaningful insights into the accountability of the decision-making arrangement as a whole. It therefore attempts to overcome the analytical difficulties by introducing a multi-level framework of analysis. This framework, in turn, can be applied with two distinct perspectives on the aims of an accountability arrangement: that of safeguarding popular control and of providing for checks and balances. The findings in each of the respective empirical chapters are interpreted from both perspectives.

Chapter 4 is the first of three empirical chapters. Each of these chapters delves into one of the three levels of comitology. Chapter 4 exclusively focuses on the system level. It analyses the development of the accountability structure that has been embedded in the comitology system from its infancy in the early 1960s to the present situation, after the entry into force of the Lisbon Treaty. Comitology was originally designed as a means for the Council of Ministers to control the Commission in its executive capacities, bypassing the Treaty of Rome. Accountability towards the European Parliament was not provided for, even though the role of Parliament was and is to operate as a controlling mechanism for the Commission's exercise of its executive capacities. Only after severe political pressure from the European Parliament did the comitology system become more and more formalized, and were limited scrutiny powers for the Parliament – and even for the Council – put in place. The chapter then takes a closer look at the reform of the comitology system following the entry into force of the Lisbon Treaty. On the basis of formal and informal documentation that circulated within the European institutions and several member states, the chapter examines more closely which forms of accountability were at stake during the negotiations on the design of the new system. The chapter concludes by identifying which accountability gaps have not yet been closed under this new system, which is likely to be fertile ground for many years of inter-institutional conflict to come.

Chapter 5 exclusively focuses on the committee level and analyses how, in practice, comitology balances the Commission's powers, and how the comitology committees are held to account by the European Parliament. The preceding chapter discussed the growth of the formal powers of the Parliament vis-à-vis comitology, but the influence of the Parliament reaches further than its formal powers only (for example, by adopting non-binding resolutions that send a clear political message to the Commission). This chapter systematically analyses the behaviour of the member state representatives in committee meetings as well as that of the Commission, and follows the chain of events within the European Parliament from mailbox to MEP. This chapter shows that the balancing of power between the Commission and the member states goes much further than envisaged in the formal design of the comitology system. The European Parliament is found to be better equipped to hold committee decision-making to account than before, but its actual behaviour is also shown to have undergone only minimal change.

Chapter 6 focuses on the accountability of the comitology committee members, whom numerous studies have found to focus less on national ties and more on the problem at hand. The participating policy specialists in many cases do not receive instructions, and they deliberate with their colleagues from the other member states and the Commission in order to find common solutions, whereas defending the national interest was and still is the core motivation underlying the comitology system as a whole. This chapter further delves into the discretionary space of the committee participants, and it measures to what degree they are actually held to account in practice. On the basis of data gathered among committee members and their superiors in Denmark and the Netherlands, it is shown that the superiors generally neither actively process information nor do they frequently or intensively discuss the input of the committee members. The superiors of the committee participants are strongly guided by what comes to their desks, tending to read written information selectively as they must cope with a high workload themselves. This also materializes in the frequency of discussions: if no written feedback is given about a certain committee meeting, the odds that the proceedings of this meeting will be discussed go down. Accountability at the national level, therefore, appears to be supply-driven instead of demand-driven: the initiative for sending information lies with the committee member, and his or her initiative alone will set an accountability process in motion.

Chapters 4 through 6 address in turn the system, committee and individual levels in comitology's multi-level accountability arrangement. In conclusion, Chapter 7 aggregates the findings of this study and places these in the context of the multi-level accountability framework presented in Chapter 3. It identifies the strengths and weaknesses in the accountability arrangements of comitology from both the popular control and the checks and balances perspective of accountability, and it locates these at the corresponding levels of aggregation. This chapter demonstrates that on the whole, the design of the accountability structure has improved over the past decades, and that some of the observed behaviours provide for very strong accountability practices. But it also draws attention to an issue that so far has been neglected in the literature on accountability: that of the failing forum. The empirical chapters show that sometimes plenty of information and a willingness to render account are available, but that the forum simply could not care less. When such practices effectively allow actors to work without restraints, forums fail. The concluding chapter thus shows that accountability deficits are not always caused by shirking agents, and it argues that assessments of the appropriateness of an accountability regime should not necessarily be made on the basis of principles that lie at the heart of over-simplified models of the workings of a bureaucracy.

2
Comitology: The System, the Committees and Their Participants

Introduction

The first chapter introduced Corné Van Alphen. Patrick Van Veen and Frits Bloem are two of his colleagues in backstage Europe, and Box 2.1 shows their work in a nutshell. Van Veen and Bloem's work is somewhat similar to that of Van Alphen's work on the Rural Development committee. The meetings are chaired by the Commission, and member state representatives attend the meetings, speak to one another and vote on implementing measures. But their work differs in some other respects. Van Alphen generally meets his European colleagues once a month, while Van Veen attends committee meetings twice as often. Van Alphen's committee allows farmers to employ certain techniques, whereas Van Veen's committee governs the market for certain agricultural products. Other committees again, which so far haven't been referred to in the examples, deal with regulation in other policy areas such as transport, research, health care, food safety and the environment. Together they vote between 2,000 and 2,500 times every year, on issues ranging from intervention stock levels of cereals to air quality regulation.

Box 2.1 Comitology in practice

> Today is a usual day in the usual meeting room in the building of DG Agriculture in Brussels. Policy specialists from all over Europe meet here to discuss the implementation of the Common Agricultural Policy. They know each other quite well, as they generally meet every fortnight and sometimes even more often. Experts Patrick Van Veen and Frits Bloem,[a] both from the Netherlands, agreed to let me join them.

> Before lunch, the Commission and the member state experts discuss a large number of technical items related to the price support of a certain agricultural product. The Commission presents its proposals, followed by critical remarks from the member state experts. Sometimes they join each other in their critique towards the Commission. They also take the floor when they believe something should be discussed that is not mentioned on the agenda.
>
> After lunch, it's voting time. 'Watch closely', Van Veen warns me, 'You will not be able to keep up with us now.' And indeed, within only a few minutes the committee rushes through five official votes related to the points discussed before lunch, after which the meeting is immediately closed. Then Van Veen turns to me smiling and says: 'You saw that? We just spent 50 million here.'
>
> [a] For reasons of anonymity, their real names have been suppressed.
> *Source*: Observation, June 2008.

The purpose of this chapter is to discuss comitology at some greater length. It is structured along the lines of the three levels of analysis that were introduced in Chapter 1 and are essential for an understanding of comitology and the relevance of accountability in relation to it. The first section discusses the *system level* of comitology. What is comitology, and why is it important? What is its function in the policy process? How many and what sorts of measures pass through the system? The second section closes in on the *committees* that together make up the comitology system. What exactly makes a committee, and how many are there? What sorts of policies do the committees handle, and how much activity do they display? And why is it so important to hold comitology committees to account? The third section focuses on the *participants within committees*. Who do the member states send to the comitology committee meetings, and in what way do they try to reach agreements? And how does accountability relate to these practices?

The comitology system

What is comitology, and what is it not?

It is not exactly clear where the word comitology comes from. Speculations on its origin range from the French expression 'kremlilogie' referring to politicized bureaucracy, to the sixteenth-century word 'comity' meaning mutual recognition of institutions between states, and to a polemic depiction of the study of the operation of public committees itself (Bergström, 2005, p. 6–7). But what it refers to in European governance is a system of committees that are composed of policy experts representing the member states and chaired by a *chef de dossier* from the Commission. They come in two sorts: 'implementing committees' and 'expert groups for delegated legislation'. Implementing committees, as the name already suggests, deal with implementing measures that are eventually adopted by the Commission. There are, however, also many cases where the Commission does not adopt separate implementing measures, but has been given the power to amend or supplement specific details of existing legislation that was previously adopted by the Council and the European Parliament. This is referred to as 'delegated legislation', and committees of member state policy experts are involved in that process as well.

The function of comitology is to 'assist' or 'control' the Commission in its executive capacities. Before the Treaty of Lisbon was adopted, there was no legal difference between the two sorts of committees and their functioning was laid down in the so-called Comitology Decisions (Council of Ministers Decisions 87/373/EEC; and 1999/468/EC, amended by 2006/512/EC). These decisions all specified a number of control procedures from which the legislator was to choose when delegating tasks to the Commission in basic legislation. Before the first Comitology Decision was adopted in 1987, such a menu was not available and committee procedures were defined, where deemed necessary, in each and every piece of legislation that delegated competences to the European Commission. A small number of these very specific procedures that were introduced before 1987 have continued to exist up to present day as their functioning has never been brought in line with the comitology Decisions (see also Chapter 4).

With the Treaty of Lisbon, the distinction between delegated legislation and implementing measures was introduced (Articles 290 and 291 TFEU), and the functions of committees in that process were renegotiated between the institutions (see Chapter 4). As further sections will show in more detail, the new regime for implementing committees is in practical terms very similar to the 'old' comitology system. More significant changes were introduced with respect to the committees dealing with delegated legislation. Since both modes involve national civil servants participating in the Commission's executive decision-making and both are further developments of the comitology system as it has always existed, this book refers to both modes together when speaking of comitology (see also Chapter 1).

Comitology, thus, only appears at the end of the policy process. It is an executive device, and hence comes into the picture when the Council of Ministers (and under co-decision also the European Parliament) has already adopted legislation. The implementation of this legislation is delegated to the Commission, and a comitology committee is simultaneously set up by the legislator to assist or control the Commission in its executive capacities (see further). Comitology committee meetings are chaired by the Commission and attended by representatives of the member states.

Comitology is not only different from other forms of committee governance in terms of institutional affiliation and confinement to executive matters, but also different in terms of its powers: many of the comitology committees have a real say over the issues they discuss. A formal vote is required from the implementing committees before the Commission can proceed to implement its policies.[1,2] If an implementing committee does not approve, the matter is referred to an appeal committee of member state representatives (until 2010, this was the Council of Ministers). Delegated legislation expert groups may also vote, but they as such do not have the power to block the Commission's proposals. Rather, the Council of Ministers and the European Parliament may do so, or they may even revoke the delegation of competences to the Commission altogether. The committees involved with delegated acts function as a signalling tool, since these two institutions use the information emanating from those groups as a basis for their judgement (Héritier et al., 2012, p. 135). This makes the 'assistance' that both types of committees provide to the Commission quite powerful.

Comitology, therefore, is a system of committees that is designed to control the executive capacities of the Commission. Even though sometimes included under the same heading,[3] the term 'comitology' does not include all other existing forms of committee governance such as preparatory expert groups or council working parties, as these either do not concern themselves with executive measures or they do not relate to the activities of the Commission. To put it in more succinct terms, comitology in this book refers to the system of committees of member state representatives which must be consulted by the Commission before it adopts executive measures, either in the form of delegated acts or implementing acts.

Comitology works on the bulk of European policies

From the aforesaid, it follows that comitology is a powerful form of committee governance. Before examining the various tasks of the individual comitology committees and the way in which they express their powers, let us first take a closer look at the relevance of the system of comitology within the European policy process. The high workload of comitology is nowadays widely recognized by many researchers of EU governance (Bergström, 2005; Christiansen and Vaccari, 2006; Franchino, 2000a, b; Neuhold, 2008; Pollack, 2003a; Vos, 1997), but surprisingly this has never been compared to that of other modes of policymaking in the European Union.[4] For that reason, fresh evidence was collected on the basis of all regulations, directives and decisions that have been adopted by the Commission, the Council and the European Parliament, and published in the Official Journal since the early 1970s.[5] It clearly shows that comitology works on the bulk of European policies.

Table 2.1 first shows the ratio of acts adopted by each institution. As mentioned previously, comitology is an executive device, which only comes into the picture at the end of the policy process. The figures show that the end of the policy process can sometimes be lengthy and may require a lot of executive measures to be adopted by the Commission. It is in this realm that the input of comitology materializes.[6]

The figures in Table 2.1 refer to the sheer amount of 'output' by the various institutions, which includes regulations, directives and decisions. In terms of content, these cannot realistically be compared, as the Commission only adopts more detailed measures on the basis of legislation adopted previously by the other institutions. What Table 2.1 does show, however, is that the Commission produces a lot of 'administrative law', and that its relevance in terms of volume must not be underestimated (Van Schendelen, 2010, p. 69–71). It is noteworthy that between 77 and 87 per cent of all EU acts adopted from 2004 through 2011 were adopted by the Commission.

Table 2.1 Regulations, directives and decisions adopted by the European institutions between 2005 and 2011

	2005	2006	2007	2008	2009	2010	2011
Parliament and Council	1.71%	3.11%	2.02%	5.29%	6.76%	4.02%	4.05%
Council alone	11.38%	13.19%	12.68%	14.98%	16.35%	15.00%	18.48%
Commission	86.90%	83.70%	85.31%	79.73%	76.89%	80.98%	77.47%
Total number of acts	3,268	3,251	2,729	2,496	2,367	2,234	2,495

Source: EUR-LEX, http://eur-lex.europa.eu, including all Decisions, Directives and Regulations, irrespective of Treaty base, adopted by the Commission or the Council exclusively, or by the co-decision procedure.

It is within this range of acts that the comitology committees have an important role to play. In some instances the Commission does act alone, but in about half of the cases it is obliged to consult a comitology committee first. Table 2.2 provides a further breakdown of the number of acts adopted by the Commission, and identifies where the adopted measures were routed via a comitology committee and where they were not.

It appears that between 45 and 60 per cent of all Commission acts are handled by comitology. In all other cases, the Commission is not subject to control by committees. For the most part, the acts over which no committee control is exercised concern decisions in the fields of agriculture and competition. Without exception, the decisions in agriculture are routine decisions, such as the continuous calculation of entry prices of crops

Table 2.2 Number of Commission acts passing through comitology

	2005	2006	2007	2008	2009	2010	2011
Via comitology	58.9%	55.8%	51.4%	47.2%	48.0%	44.5%	46.4%
Comitology committees working under 1999/2006 Decisions	57.4%	54.1%	50.2%	46.1%	46.4%	42.8%	19.1%
Comitology committees not working under Comitology Decisions	1.5%	1.7%	1.2%	1.1%	1.6%	1.5%	1.2%
Implementing act committees working under 2011 Regulation	–	–	–	–	–	–	25.9%
Delegated act expert groups (post-Lisbon)	–	–	–	–	–	0.2%	0.2%
Not via comitology	41.1%	44.2%	48.6%	52.8%	52.0%	55.5%	53.6%
Agriculture	22.6%	22.4%	21.9%	25.0%	28.2%	29.6%	24.7%
Competition	12.1%	15.1%	19.1%	19.5%	15.5%	16.4%	17.4%
Fisheries	2.0%	2.4%	3.9%	4.3%	2.9%	3.0%	4.8%
Miscellaneous	4.4%	4.3%	3.7%	4.0%	5.4%	6.5%	6.7%
Total number of acts adopted by the Commission	2,840	2,721	2,328	1,990	1,820	1,809	1,932

Source: EUR-LEX. Numbers found by counting how many times an opinion or consultation of a committee was referred to under 'whereas' in all acts adopted by the Commission, irrespective of Treaty base (dataset extracted from EUR-LEX by Sietse Ringers).[7]

entering the European market given world market prices and exchange rates and the granting of import licenses. In competition, decisions relate to declaring business concentrations compatible with the common market, and decisions of the Commission not to oppose mergers. Although the percentage of non-controlled decisions appears to have risen over the last years, this is only a statistical artefact. The total number of Commission acts, and in fact of all Union acts, has been declining over this period as a result of, mainly, the simplification of the Common Agricultural Policy (see also Figure 1.1 in Chapter 1). The number of non-committee controlled acts is comparatively stable in absolute terms, because most of these must be taken as a matter of routine. The number of other acts is more variable.

These figures show that the comitology system is one of the most important governance tools in the European Union, measured by the volume of work that it deals with. But in terms of the importance of the acts discussed in the comitology committees, the matters they discuss are of a different nature from those discussed in the Council and the European Parliament. Still, these matters can be very important and affect European citizens and business directly. For example, when an animal disease such as avian flu breaks out, measures need to be taken such as transport bans, disinfection schemes and vaccination programmes or prohibitions. Sometimes all livestock needs to be exterminated in certain areas, which has a huge societal impact. All these matters are worked out through comitology.[8] The same is true for an effort to integrate all national airspaces into a Single European Sky in order to reduce mid-air collision risks and to increase air traffic management efficiency for civil aviation. This requires a range of work programmes, decisions and regulations to integrate air traffic management systems. However, because the military uses air space as well, it, too, is affected by this policy. The comitology committee for the Single European Sky thus deals with very technical implementation matters, but these are politically very salient because the issues directly touch upon national sovereignty.[9]

These are just a couple of examples, but there are thousands of such decisions that may seem quite technical at first sight, but that do have political salience. These are all covered in administrative acts adopted by the Commission, which account for the bulk of the regulations, directives and decisions that are adopted in the European Union. Between 45 and 60 per cent of these Commission acts are first submitted to one of these committees of member state representatives before they are finally adopted. These committees are in a position to approve proposed measures, to refer them to an appeal body of member states, or to supply information to the Council and the European Parliament which can block the proposed measures on that basis. All this enables them to control the Commission and influence its policies.

Let us now take a look at the committees that together form the comitology system. How many comitology committees are there, what do they do, and why do we need to bother about their accountability?

Comitology committees

Officially 259; in practice, 219 committees

There are different counts of the number of comitology committees. The highest estimates are by Toeller and Van Schendelen, who respectively arrive at 418 and about 450 (Toeller, 2002, p. 315; Van Schendelen, 2006, 31). Over the past few years, until the split between delegated act groups and implementing act groups took effect, the Commission has steadily reported the existence of about 250 committees (European Commission, 2006, 2007, 2008, 2009a, 2010b, 2011a). The trick here is mainly in the definition. Easy as it may appear, there are actually a lot of issues to take into account when defining what a comitology committee is (Toeller, 2002, p. 313–22).

Legal instruments and actual committees: The Commission counts the number of committees by the number that has formally been set up under one of the Comitology Decisions (Council Decisions 1987/373/EEC, 1999/468/EC and 2006/512/EC, Council and European Parliament Regulation 2011/182/EU). A different approach is to count the number of times legislation mentions (and hence installs) a comitology committee for overseeing its implementation. Often, new legislation assigns this task to committees that already exist for overseeing the implementation of a closely related file. Counts of legal instruments that establish committees are thus always considerably higher than the number of committees that exist in practice.

Lost in alignment: Before the first Comitology Decision was adopted in 1987 to establish common rules for the functioning of committees, each piece of basic legislation specified its own committee procedures, which lead to a jungle of different procedures. The 1987 Decision, and later the 1999 and 2006 Decisions, provided a template for establishing new committees, but the procedures of the committees set up prior to 1987 were only gradually brought into line with those common rules. This process in fact still has not been completed even with the entry into force of the 2011 Regulation on implementing acts, which aligned most but not all of the remaining comitology committees. The Commission, however, only produces statistics on the committees working under the ordinary regime, so that several committees are not listed in official reports. After the 2011 reform, only four non-aligned committees remain: the Advisory Committee on State Aid (which may recommend its opinions to be published in the Official Journal); the Advisory Committee on Restrictive Practices and Dominant Positions; the Advisory Committee on Concentrations; and the Advisory Committee on Safety, Hygiene and Health Protection at Work. None of these, however, seemed active in 2011.

Sections and configurations: Several committees are divided into subcommittees, known as sections or configurations. The Standing Committee on the Food Chain and Animal Health is an example of this. It has sections on, among others, animal welfare, biological safety of the food chain, animal nutrition and toxicological safety. These sections have a permanent status, just as any 'regular' committee has. In fact, there is nothing apart from their name that would make them any different from other comitology committees. In a material sense, these are ordinary committees, but they do not appear in the Commission's formal counts of the number of committees.

Working groups: Some committees have set up working groups to pre-discuss issues before the 'official' committee meetings. These can have a permanent or an ad hoc status. The actual committee opinions are expressed in the official committee meetings. Hence, these working groups cannot be regarded as committees.

Combined meetings: In some cases, committee meetings are combined – that is, meetings for Committee A may be scheduled and immediately followed by some points regarding Committee B. The participants in the meeting remain the same. This procedure is especially common in committees that have only a few issues to discuss and whose issues are closely related to those discussed in another committee. For example, two committees that used to merge their meetings were the Management Committee of Sugar (DG Agriculture)[10] and the Management Committee on Horizontal Issues regarding Processed Agricultural Products Not Listed in Annex 1 (DG Enterprise) which mainly deals with biscuits and soft drinks. The same participants simply discuss another issue under another committee name. Despite the overlap, these cases should be treated separately. The meetings of these committees are not necessarily always merged and the nature of the issues their participants discuss may also be different.

Written procedure: Sometimes, the Commission asks the member state representatives to give a formal opinion by post or email rather than in a committee meeting. This is known as the 'written procedure'. In effect, it has all the elements of a committee meeting except for the meeting itself. The actual use of the written procedure is limited. There are only very few committees that never meet but exclusively use the written procedure. Still, these can be considered to be committees in the sense that they have to be consulted and their opinions have to be taken into account.

Inactive committees: Some committees have not met for years, nor have they ever made use of the written procedure. They only continue to exist for the record, and may be revived whenever there is a need to convene a meeting, for example, when certain implementing rules expire. Inactive committees do sometimes remain on the Commission's budget, which raises the count of committees (Toeller, 2002, p. 313–22).

Incomplete registration for delegated act expert groups: Since 2002, the Commission has published annual reports on the activity of comitology committees, and it continues to do so for the committees under the implementing act regime. For the delegated act expert groups, this rich data source is not available. The Commission has adopted a policy of disclosing the names of all existing expert groups including those dealing with delegated acts via an Internet register (European Commission, 2010a), but in practice it does not appear complete. Because the Commission has agreed with the Council to consult a delegated act expert group for every delegated act to be adopted (see Chapter 4), we do have a picture of the number of acts passing through this part of comitology. It is not clear, however, how many different committees are involved for delegated legislation.

Table 2.3 shows the total number of active comitology committees. These figures were found by taking the number of committees mentioned in the Commission's Annex to the annual Comitology Reports, adding the number of subsections that act as self-containing committees, subtracting the number committees that appeared to be inactive and adding the number of active committees not included in the annual reports.[11]

Comitology committees deal with a wide range of issues

The topics that are discussed in comitology committee meetings vary enormously. Comitology deals with a very broad range of policy issues and covers these in detail: from 'seeds and propagating material for agriculture, horticulture and forestry' to 'reciprocal recognition of national

Table 2.3 Number of comitology committees

	2005	2006	2007	2008	2009	2010	2011
Number of comitology committees reported by the Commission	250	279	269	270	266	259	268
Sections and configurations acting as comitology committees	43	40	39	43	36	40	36
Inactive comitology committees	68	75	79	77	82	77	89
Number of delegated act expert groups	0	0	0	0	0	1	2
Number of active non-aligned committees	5	6	5	5	7	4	0
Total number of active comitology committees	230	250	234	241	227	227	219

Source: Commission Staff Working Documents accompanying the Reports from the Commission on the working of committees during 2005 through 2010 (European Commission, 2006, 2007, 2008, 2009a, 2010b, 2011a, 2012), also including the data reported under Table 2.2 in order to count the number of active non-aligned committees. In 2010, only four delegated acts were adopted, all in the same issue area, all on the same day. In 2011, three delegated acts were adopted on two days in two issue areas. The number of active delegated act expert groups is thus set at one and two for 2010 and 2011, respectively.

boat masters' certificates for the carriage of goods and passengers by inland waterway'. Within these often very specific domains, the draft implementation measures discussed by the committees can be about norm-setting, action programmes, funding, market management, authorization for products, etc. They can, for example, determine the black list of air carriers that are banned in the European Union[12] or discuss what specific uses of genetically modified organisms are allowed.[13]

Box 2.2 Excerpt from the Patients' Rights Directive (2011/24/EU)

> Whereas:
> [...]
> (61) It is of particular importance that, when empowered to adopt delegated acts in accordance with Article 290 TFEU, the Commission carry out appropriate consultations during its preparatory work, including at expert level.
> [...]

Article 12
[...]
5. The Commission shall adopt the measures referred to in paragraph 4(a) by means of delegated acts in accordance with Article 17 and subject to the conditions of Articles 18 and 19. The measures referred to in points (b) and (c) of paragraph 4 shall be adopted in accordance with the regulatory procedure referred to in Article 16(2).
[...]
Article 16
1. The Commission shall be assisted by a Committee, consisting of representatives of the Member States and chaired by the Commission representative.
2. Where reference is made to this paragraph, Articles 5 and 7 of Decision 1999/468/EC shall apply, having regard to the provisions of Article 8 thereof.

The specific issues about which the committees are supposed to have a say depends on the initial legislation that is adopted by the Council of Ministers (and under co-decision, also by Parliament). Box 2.2 shows an example of this. It is an excerpt from the Patients' Rights Directive: an effort to safeguard patients' rights in cross-border health care. Article 16 establishes a committee. The reference to Decision 1999/468/EC in Article 16.2 makes it a comitology committee. It specifies which voting procedure applies in the Patients' Rights Committee (see further). Furthermore, recital number 61 underlines a political commitment of the Commission to make 'expert consultations' before the adoption of any delegated act. This also includes the consultation of a member state expert committee (see Chapter 4). Article 16.2 and recital 61 specify control mechanisms for the adoption of delegated and implementing acts.

All other references in this piece of legislation to either delegated acts, or to Article 16.2, specify what control mechanism applies in what cases. Article 12.5, stipulates that all measures listed in Article 12.4a are to be taken by means of delegated acts, and that those in Article 12.4b and 12.4c must be regulated through implementing acts. These two articles lay down that networks of health-care providers and expertise centres are to be established, and that the two committees are to specifically define what a network is, and that they are to discuss the criteria these networks have to fulfil.

Comitology committees can continue to exist until a policy is fully implemented, for example when a four-year programme is finalized that is not supposed to continue after the four years have elapsed. For certain policies, however, implementation is never finished. The Common Agricultural Policy, for example, is about continuous market management for a range of agricultural products. Its committees sometimes meet on a weekly basis, and some have been doing so for decades. The tasks that committees have should therefore not necessarily be seen as 'one-offs'. Rather, it depends on the subject as to whether a matter is dealt with only once or continuously.

Powers of the committees depend on member state preferences

The comitology committees deal with a very broad range of issues. As was briefly mentioned earlier, some committees do so by means of binding votes on Commission proposals for executive measures (Article 291 TFEU), whereas others merely provide information, on the basis of which the Council and the European Parliament may decide to veto particular measures or to revoke delegated powers to the Commission altogether (Article 290 TFEU). Taken together, the committee system includes six different procedures, and these mainly specify whether a vote is required, and if so, how many votes the Commission needs in order to have its proposals accepted, or whether the proposals should instead be referred to an appeal committee.[14] The basic legislation, which spells out exactly what measures need to be adopted by the Commission, specifies which of the procedures applies in which particular cases.

Five out of these six procedures apply to 'implementing committees', working under Article 291 (TFEU).[15] When the *advisory procedure* is used, committees give their opinion on Commission proposals through a simple majority vote by member states. The Commission is allowed to ignore the opinion of the committee, although it is supposed to give 'the utmost' consideration to the expressed position. Any constraint upon the Commission is therefore purely informal.

The *examination procedure* is a bit more constraining. Here, the Commission can always proceed with implementation unless there is a qualified majority of member states or a simple majority of committee members against a draft measure. In those cases, adoption of the proposed measure is suspended and the Commission may choose between resubmitting a revised version of the draft measure to the same committee within two months (and thus risking a new rejection) or forwarding the same measure to an appeal body of member states within one month. The appeal committee has slightly different voting rules: only a qualified majority against can block the Commission here. Before the 2010 overhaul of the comitology system, this procedure was known as the 'management procedure', although before 2010 the Council of Ministers was used for appeals and simple majorities of committee members could not block the adoption of draft measures in first instance. Typically, the examination procedure is used when it comes to managing or approving the budget of a continuing work programme. Examples of this include the Framework Programmes for research and the Common Agricultural Policy.

There is also a *regulatory variant to the examination procedure* that used to be known as the 'regulatory procedure' prior to the 2010 reform. This procedure is the same as the examination procedure presented earlier, but in this case the Commission can be blocked in first instance by a blocking minority instead of a qualified or simple majority. Thereafter, the procedure is the same as in the standard examination procedure: either resubmission of an amended draft to the same committee within two months, or forwarding of the blocked draft measure to the appeal committee which, in turn, can only block the adoption of the proposed measures by means of a qualified majority against.[16] This variant applies by default to all policies that relate to financial services, taxation and health, and is optional for any other piece of legislation.

Two special procedures apply to three categories of issues within the common commercial policy. For definitive anti-dumping measures and countervailing measures, there is an *external trade variant to the examination procedure*. Here, a simple majority against does not allow the Commission to choose between revision and resubmission or referral to the appeal committee, but obliges the Commission to consult the member states, and inform the members of the original committee of the results of those consultations, but to let the appeal committee decide on the draft measure. For multilateral safeguard measures, there is another exceptional procedure. In this case, the regulatory variant to the examination procedure applies, but the appeal committee, too, can block the Commission by means of a blocking minority. This is the *safeguard variant to the examination procedure*.

The final procedure concerns *delegated legislation*. The delegated act 'expert group' is to be consulted immediately before the Commission formally proposes its delegated act to the European Parliament and the Council (see Chapter 4). It is up to the Commission to decide whether or not rules of procedure apply to the expert groups. According to the standard model of these rules provided by the Commission, the expert groups are to reach consensus, although voting by means of a simple majority is also possible (European Commission, 2010a, 15). No consequences are provided in the rules of procedure in the case of a negative vote, which means that this voting procedure, when used at all, is similar to the advisory procedure for implementing acts. Following consultation of the 'expert group', the Commission sends its final draft-delegated measure to the Council and the European Parliament, which under normal circumstances both have between two and four months to oppose the Commission's proposed measure. In order to assist these institutions in their scrutiny, the Commission forwards documents stemming from the 'expert consultations' to them (European Parliament, Council of Ministers and Commission, 2011).

Prior to 2010, the 'regulatory procedure with scrutiny' was applied in such cases, which differed from the current situation in two important respects: the Council and the European Parliament were not able to revoke the Commission's delegated legislative powers, and the committees that currently act as expert groups voted by means of a qualified majority, in much the same way as in the current regulatory variant to the examination procedure. Following the entry into force of the Lisbon Treaty, an alignment process started for the committees that hitherto used the regulatory procedure with scrutiny. One by one, their procedures will be aligned to the delegated act system, which will take a number of years to complete.[17,18]

There is an extensive body of literature on voting procedures in comitology committees, in which many more specificities of these procedures are discussed.[19] There are two observations that matter at this particular point. First, it is evident that the aforementioned procedures vary in the degree to which the member states exercise control over the Commission. Apparently the member states feel the need to control the Commission, which is the very point of comitology, but some procedures make it easier or harder for the Commission to get its way.

Second, following from this, the question of which voting procedure to apply in a specific case is a matter of deliberate choice. Even though the European Parliament and the Council co-decide on legislation, it is particularly the Council that tends to insist on strong voting procedures in order to control the Commission (Bergström, 2005, p. 221–6). Under the present Treaty this involves choosing between delegated legislation and implementation committees, setting up a committee, and in the case of implementing acts, specifying voting procedures for particular issues. As a result, in some cases, the Commission has more leeway than in others, but that is because the legislative institutions, and the

Council in particular, have made deliberate choices (Blom-Hansen, 2011a, 610; Bergström, Farrell and Héritier, 2007). It thus follows from these two observations that the importance attributed by member states to individual issues varies, also when it comes to executive measures that stem from basic legislation that has been passed by the Council itself. The fact that there are different voting rules for comitology committees indicates that the member states attribute different levels of political importance to the issues the committees deal with. In some cases, the Commission needs the backing of a qualified majority of member states in order to get its measures accepted by a comitology committee; in other cases it only needs to be sure that no simple or qualified majority explicitly votes against. Sometimes, it only needs to consider the opinion of the committee; in other cases, it may be threatened by a veto from the Council or the European Parliament on the basis of information stemming from committee deliberations. In any event, issues that are more salient to the member states are subject to stronger procedures (Franchino, 2000b).

Committee activity is not randomly spread over policy sectors

The committees are not randomly spread across Commission DGs. Some DGs host more committees than others. Also, not all committees are equally active, both in terms of their frequency of meeting and in the number of times they vote. Table 2.4 shows how many committees exist per Commission DG, thus representing issue areas, and how often they meet.

The 219 committees together convened 786 meetings in 2011. Table 2.4 also shows that over half of all committees are found under the DGs of Agriculture, Environment, Health, Mobility and Transport, and Enterprise and Industry. These five clusters together also account for just over half of all committee meetings across all policy sectors. The number of meetings is particularly high in the DG of Agriculture. This is mainly due to the Common Agricultural Policy, for which 18 committees frequently meet to vote on the handling of the markets of specific products. One of these, namely the Management Committee for the Common Organisation of Agricultural Markets, met a staggering 76 times in 2011.[20]

Output of comitology committees

Another indicator of the activity of comitology committees is the number of times the committees vote. This is, essentially, the output that the implementing committees deliver. Table 2.5 lists the number

Table 2.4 Committees per Commission DG in 2011

Commission DG	Number of active committees	Number of meetings per year	Average number of meetings per year per committee
Agriculture and Rural Development	18	142	7.89
Anti-Fraud Office	1	3	3
Budget	1	4	4
Climate Action	3	14	4.67
Communication	1	1	1
Economic and Financial Affairs	0	0	0
Education and Culture	6	18	3
Employment, Social Affairs and Inclusion	2	3	1.5
Energy	8	13	1.63
Enlargement	3	8	2.67
Enterprise and Industry	23	56	2.43
Environment	21	43	2.05
EuropeAid	6	17	2.83
Foreign Policy Instruments	2	4	2
Health and Consumers	25	146	5.84
Home Affairs	7	24	3.43
Humanitarian and Civil Protection	2	5	2.5
Informatics	1	2	2
Information Society and Media	5	20	4
Internal Market	7	18	2.57
Justice	6	6	1
Maritime Affairs and Fisheries	2	9	4.5
Mobility and Transport	19	53	2.79
Regional Policy	1	5	5
Research	17	61	3.59
Secretariat-General	1	1	1
Statistics	7	14	2
Taxation and Customs Union	18	81	4.5
Trade	6	15	2.5
Total	**219**	**786**	**3.59**

Note: Not including the appeal committee which convened five times. The two expert groups for delegated acts have been counted as having one meeting each under DG Environment (see Table 2.3).
Source: European Commission (2012).

Table 2.5 Committee activity per Commission DG in 2011

Commission DG	Number of votes	Average number of votes per meeting	Number of matters referred to the Council or appeal committee
Agriculture and Rural Development	271	1.91	0
Anti-Fraud Office	0	0	0
Budget	1	0.25	0
Climate Action	10	0.71	0
Communication	6	6	0
Economic and Financial Affairs	0	0	0
Education and Culture	100	5.56	0
Employment, Social Affairs and Inclusion	11	3.67	0
Energy	15	1.15	0
Enlargement	58	7.25	0
Enterprise and Industry	59	1.05	0
Environment	58	1.35	0
EuropeAid	128	7.53	0
Foreign Policy Instruments	2	0.5	0
Health and Consumers	625	4.28	12
Home Affairs	33	1.38	0
Humanitarian and Civil Protection	15	3	0
Informatics	1	0.5	0
Information Society and Media	41	2.05	0
Internal Market	13	0.72	0
Justice	14	2.33	0
Maritime Affairs and Fisheries	23	2.56	0
Mobility and Transport	65	1.23	0
Regional Policy	6	1.20	0
Research	206	3.38	0
Secretariat-General	1	1	0
Statistics	11	0.79	0
Taxation and Customs Union	84	1.04	0
Trade	6	0.40	0
Total	**1,868**	**2.38**	**12**

Note: The expert groups for delegated acts has been counted as voting three times under DG Environment (see Table 2.3).
Source: European Commission (2012).

of times votes were cast in 2011 (as aggregated per Commission DG), the average number of votes per meeting, and the number of times the outcome of the vote was such that the matter had to be referred to the Council of Ministers or to the appeal committee. Since it is not clear if there were votes on the three delegated acts adopted in 2011, the total number of delegated acts is counted, as this refers to the number of matters dealt with by the committee.

The DG of Health and Consumer Affairs heads the list with 625 votes cast in 2011, with the Standing Committee on Medicinal Products for Human Use in this DG accounting for a full 237 of these votes. Another striking observation is that, of the 1,868 votes that were cast, only 12 matters were referred to the appeal committee.[21] This means that the outcome of the vote is practically always such that the Commission can adopt its measures right away. It would be wrong to assume, however, that the member state representatives generally tend to agree with anything the Commission proposes. The agendas of the committee meetings show that most points on the agenda are for an 'exchange of views'. These are preliminary discussions in which the Commission receives feedback on future executive measures, which the Commission will only formally table for voting when it can be sure of a majority in the committee (Alfé, Brandsma and Christiansen, 2009, p. 145–6). If issues have been hashed out in advance, taking a vote can sometimes be a matter of seconds, as the case of Van Veen and Bloem in Box 2.1 demonstrates.

Practices within comitology committees

In principle, the member states are completely free to decide about whom to send to a comitology committee meeting. Typically, however, the member states are represented by policy specialists working within ministries or in agencies to which the management of a particular policy has been delegated. It is not uncommon for member state delegations to consist of an official spokesman plus one or more colleagues from other ministries or agencies. Usually the EEA countries and acceding countries have the right to observe the meeting without participating.[22]

The Commission has committed itself to making the attendance lists and several other documents related to committee meetings available through online registers of comitology documents.[23] Still, the attendance lists do not disclose the names of the members of the committees. These lists usually mention the names of the relevant Commission officials, but only the organizational entities of the members attending on behalf of the member states are shown. Names and addresses are not disclosed. The Commission argues it is not in a position to do so, because of the regulations on the protection of personal data (see further in Council and European Parliament Regulation 1049/2001/EC).

But even within the member states it is often unknown who exactly is a member of the committees. Chapters 5 and 6 of this book show that in the cases of Denmark and the Netherlands no lists of members are available, sometimes not even within ministries or agencies. Similarly, Beyers and Bursens observe a lack of attention for comitology within Belgian ministries, which they attribute to a lack of political interest at the federal level (Beyers and Bursens, 2006, p. 182–4).

Thus far, this chapter has argued that committee members not only use their power at the moment they vote, but that they can also express their approval or concerns when discussing issues in the committees in the shadow of a future vote in the case of implementing acts, or of European Parliament or Council opposition when delegated legislation is concerned. The Commission can then anticipate and change its proposals, and the member state representatives can reconsider their negotiation strategies if necessary. The ways in which these discussions take place are the subject of a lively academic debate on interaction styles between committee participants. By now, a fair number of empirical studies have been conducted on this matter. In general, the outcomes of these studies can be summarized under two headings: intergovernmental bargaining and supranational deliberation (Pollack, 2003a; Krapohl and Zurek, 2006; Blom-Hansen and Brandsma, 2009). These approaches deliver different reasons as to the importance of accountability of committee participants.

Intergovernmental bargaining: Defending the national interest

The origin of comitology shows that the system is meant to be a control device for member states over the Commission. By inserting comitology clauses in new legislative acts, the Council subjects the Commission to scrutiny by committees of member state representatives. These representatives vote on draft implementation measures, or advise on draft-delegated legislation, on the basis of which the Council (and the European Parliament) can step in at a later stage.

It is this line of argument that is central to the intergovernmental bargaining approach. It states that comitology effectively shares some basic characteristics with the Council of Ministers in what used to be known as the first pillar: the Commission has the right of initiative; the member states participate in the decision-making process; and the power of each respective member state is expressed in the weight of their vote in the implementation committees, or in the shadow of a vote in the Council when it concerns delegated legislation. Therefore, the structure of the bargaining arena is similar to that of the Council (Moravcsik, 1998). Hence comitology can be seen as an arena of intergovernmental negotiation – even more so in the case of implementation committees which vote themselves.

The research pointing towards intergovernmental negotiation in comitology committees primarily focuses on voting procedures within the committees. It is mainly of a game-theoretical nature, and in terms of institutional preferences, it confirms the constraining power of the member states over the Commission (e.g. Steunenberg, Koboldt and Schmidtchen, 1996; Franchino, 2000b; Ballmann, Epstein and O'Halloran, 2002; Pollack, 2003b). Several case studies present similar conclusions, as these observe tough negotiation and strategic use of voting rules (Bradley, 1998; Philip, 1998; Daemen and Van Schendelen, 1998). From the perspective of intergovernmental bargaining, the committee participants behave exactly as they are formally expected to do: they act as member state representatives pursuing their own national interests. That the committee participants truly promote the national interest instead of another interest (possibly disguised as being 'national'), however, is only assumed. Accountability is essential to safeguard against non-national interests getting the upper hand in the input of the committee participants.

Supranational deliberation: Consensual discussions between well-intentioned experts

Supranational deliberation challenges this view of comitology. Many case studies, and also some larger-scale surveys, reveal that in practice member state representatives do not bargain intensely to secure their own national interests. Rather, the interaction between committee members, and the Commission is characterized by deliberation between experts aimed at solving common problems.

The prime advocates of the deliberative approach, Joerges and Neyer (1997a, b), see this expert-driven mode of decision-making as a solution to a legitimacy problem. The core of their argument is that nation states 'have very few mechanisms ensuring that "foreign" identities and their interests be taken into account within their decision-making processes. The legitimacy of supranational institutions can be designed as a cure to these deficiencies – as a correction of "nation-state failures" as it were' (Joerges and Neyer, 1997a, 293). This is especially important for policies related to European market regulation. While the Commission has competences to regulate the European market, comitology can serve as a forum for transnational and supranational dialogue. From this perspective, a committee system in which civil servants from all member states try to find common solutions is a very good thing. It forces the participants to take into account the positions of other member states (Neyer, 2000; Joerges, 2006, 795).

Apart from the previous study, there is a range of empirical studies that show that in practice, committees are in fact used for deliberation among experts. The meetings are characterized by a spirit of expertise, and scientific evidence plays a prominent role in the committees' deliberations (Wessels, 1998, 225; Dehousse, 2003, 803). Finding the best *technical* solution is what is most important to many participants, who also feel a strong allegiance to their own professional background (Egeberg, Schäfer and Trondal, 2003, 32; Sannerstedt, 2005, p. 105). There is also a substantial body of literature on the socialization effect of participating in European committees. It shows that committee participants internalize European norms so that they become increasingly willing to pursue the common European good, transcending the national interest (Beyers and Dierickx, 1998; Egeberg, 1999; Trondal, 2002; Egeberg, Schäfer and Trondal, 2003; Beyers and Trondal, 2004).

Another argument for the supranational deliberation approach is that the national interest is only a relative notion. Observational evidence suggests that 'national positions' can be formulated on the basis of a position taken by the national parliament, but they may equally well result from ad hoc coordination with several selected colleagues working on related files (Geuijen et al., 2008, 129–49). Other studies show that many committee participants do not receive instructions on what positions to take in the committee meetings, and that sometimes they mix roles between government representative and independent expert (Geuijen et al., 2008, 129–49; Egeberg, Schäfer and Trondal, 2003; Sannerstedt, 2005).

However, these findings raise the question of who keeps track of the committee members. Even though the legitimacy of the eventual policies is fostered because foreign interests are taken into account, comitology effectively produces acts that are eventually binding for the general public. It risks empowering the executive (Joerges, 2004). Hence the accountability of comitology is a relevant matter. But the evidence demonstrates that the accountability of committee members, which is implied in intergovernmental bargaining-inspired work, may not simply be assumed to be present.

Box 2.3 Balancing national and European interests

On his way back from lunch, Frits Bloem[a] answers a phone call and takes some steps away. Patrick Van Veen[a] explains to me that it is a colleague from The Hague telling Bloem which requests for price support by agricultural businesses were forwarded to the Commission from Holland. The deadline for this had passed only moments before, and the Commission works out its subsidy proposal over lunch. This is a matter of routine at every meeting of this committee. The phone call gives Bloem the opportunity to do a last-minute check to see if the Commission got its figures right before the committee votes on the subsidy proposal. 'And', Van Veen adds, 'I don't want to know.'

Van Veen is convinced he should stake his position on macro-economic grounds only and should not be influenced by any national interest. Otherwise, there could be arguments in the committee if even a bit more subsidy funds would be awarded to a particular country in order to benefit its national industry. To Van Veen, that is both speculation and preferential treatment, which has nothing to do with the management of the common market.

Therefore, Van Veen and Bloem have divided their tasks. Van Veen is the official Dutch spokesperson, but he does not know the details of any particular Dutch application. Bloem does, and he checks the data prior to the vote. Only after the meeting closes (see Box 2.1) does Van Veen curiously ask his colleague if any Dutch applications were awarded.

[a] For reasons of anonymity, their real names have been suppressed.
Source: Observation, June 2008.

Comitology: Why bother about its accountability?

The earlier discussion might give the impression that comitology amounts to much ado about nothing spectacular. Taking the example of the Patients' Rights directive again, we see that the political decision to establish patients' rights for cross-border health care had already been taken by political actors. The committee only discusses what *specifically* makes a health-care network. Why would we need to care about its accountability, then, if comitology is 'only' about the nitty-gritty work of implementation?

There are several reasons. The first is that such seemingly small, technical issues still bear political salience (Radaelli, 1999, 758–62).

For example, the Habitats directive, which also makes use of a committee procedure, protects environmental sites and species by specifying that any action directly or indirectly affecting these should be refrained from, or should be compensated. The list of sites and species is decided upon through a committee. It goes without saying that the issue of listing can easily become politicized, for example, if some odd members of an endangered species show up near an infrastructural project that is about to be started. The Habitats directive is formulated strictly enough to block infrastructural projects that fail to provide environmental compensation, or of which the environmental effects have not been properly investigated. But even when such issues are not politicized, they can still be interesting. To those who are directly affected by new legislation, the devil is usually not in the objectives of legislation but rather in the details of implementation (Van Schendelen and Scully, 2006, 6).

The other reasons have to do with the raison d'être of comitology itself. In order to understand this, a brief look at history is necessary at this point. When the first acts of the European communities were to be implemented by the Commission in the early 1960s, the member states felt that the Commission should not have too much discretion in doing so. What if this 'new' supranational institution were to act against the preferences of the member states? Comitology was invented as a way out of the discussion on control. For legislation for which the member states felt the need to do so, the Council imposed the condition upon the Commission that it must consult committees composed of representatives from the national administrations before adopting executive measures. If the committee were to voice a negative opinion, the proposed measure would be handed over to the Council. In this way, the Commission would be controlled in exercising its executive capacities without jeopardizing the contents of the Treaty.[24] The Council simply delegated implementation to the Commission as it should, but it imposed a condition in doing so. Subsequent discussions on member state control over the Commission's implementation powers could thus be recast into discussions on stricter or looser voting procedures within the comitology committees, without having the need to reopen the entire Pandora's box (Haibach, 2000; Blom-Hansen, 2008). Hence, comitology can partly be understood as an accountability mechanism that aims to keep the Commission in check.

The third reason is related to this. Even though the European Parliament gained co-decision powers as from the Maastricht treaty, comitology has to a great extent remained an exclusive member state affair. The European Parliament worried that, in case of disagreement between the Council and Parliament, implementing rules would hollow out existing legislation because of Parliament's absence from the comitology system (Bradley, 1997).

Finally, the accountability of the committee members is important because it is a vital element in the position of the member states vis-à-vis the Commission (Brandsma, 2010a). The key reason why comitology committees exist at all was, and still is, because the member states recognize the power of executive measures and don't want to give the Commission carte blanche. Even though the literature on intergovernmental bargaining presents some evidence that comitology indeed promotes the interests of member states, a large number of studies also indicate that the members of these committees are in practice to some extent detached from their national ties. The participants are policy specialists who, in many cases, receive no instructions, but deliberate with their colleagues from the other member states and the Commission in order to find common solutions. In practice, their interaction style in committee meetings has very little to do with defending the national interest, whereas defending the national interest was and still is the core motivation underlying the comitology system as a whole (Blom-Hansen, 2011a, b). This, too, makes accountability important.

In this way, multiple accountability issues are at play at the same time: the accountability of the Commission by means of comitology, the accountability of comitology decision-making as such, and the accountability of those attending the comitology committee meetings. This involves issues at the system level, which concerns its institutional set-up, as well as issues at the committee level and the participant level, which concern the degree to which the accountability norms specified in the set-up of the system are actually put into practice.

This chapter has presented what comitology is and what people like Van Alphen, Bloem and Van Veen do when they are in Brussels. Comitology is involved in 45–60 per cent of all regulations, directives and decisions adopted by the Commission, which amounts to 36–52 per cent of *all* acts adopted by the institutions together. Comitology is the default option for dealing with executive matters. Mostly, it is necessary for the Commission to consult a comitology committee before it can adopt measures. Comitology deals with a lot of low politics, as it primarily concerns the technical aspects of policies. Even though comitology only deals with executive matters as opposed to new basic legislation, the matters it discusses are eventually binding for the general public, which makes accountability important – particularly for a decision-making mode that works on such a large number of measures.

This system of about 220 committees, dealing with a large variety of topics and issuing around 2,000 opinions a year, has grown to be a considerable decision-maker in its own right.

But how can accountability be gauged in a complex system like comitology? Chapter 3 demonstrates that the challenge for the accountability of a multi-level governance setting such as comitology is to have an accountability arrangement that is also truly multi-level. In the case of comitology, this comes down to three elements: accountability at the system level, which refers to the accountability relationships foreseen in the decision-making processes of comitology; accountability at the committee level, in which the individual committees act as actors or as forums; and at the level of individual committee participants within their home organizations within the member states. The next chapter shows how these three levels are interlinked, and how they can be disaggregated so as to allow for empirical analysis.

3
Accountability and Multi-Level Governance

Introduction

Multi-level governance structures are mushrooming in the European Union to the extent that some nowadays speak of a European administrative 'space' (Hofmann, 2008; Egeberg and Trondal, 2009). Next to comitology, through which 2,000 to 2,500 measures are adopted each and every year, there is also a wide range of other, sometimes called 'new' administrative arrangements that include a fusion of both national- and European-level administrators. These include, for instance, national agencies and regulators allying together in networks that bypass national governments, sometimes under the auspices of the Commission; national experts, civil servants and more stakeholders who provide input to the Commission through its expert groups or open coordination systems; and member state civil servants preparing Council negotiations in its many working parties.

It is often argued that multi-level governance settings like these lack accountability, but to date it has proven remarkably hard to observe empirically whether this really is the case. Much of the research on this matter exclusively focuses on either European or national lines of accountability, more or less ignoring the essential aspect of multi-level governance in the set-up of the analysis: its fusion of administrative layers. This feature requires a more complex analytical framework in order to capture the accountability of the full governance arrangement.

This chapter sets out to come to terms with the concept of accountability in an analytical sense, and gradually works towards a sophisticated framework of analysis that is tailored to multi-level governance settings. The first section of this chapter defines accountability and discusses its relevance. What does accountability mean, and what desiderata is accountability supposed to contribute to? This section, therefore, discusses the meaning of accountability, as well as normative benchmarks that can be used to assess its functioning.

The second section hones in on key issues for analysing accountability in a multi-level context. Who is to be held to account by whom, and for what? This section demonstrates that the literature on multi-level accountability mainly argues that it is very hard, if not impossible, to have any accountability in multi-level governance settings at all, if only for theoretical reasons. However, I argue that it is possible to move beyond this deadlock. Taking a slightly less traditionalist approach towards who should render account to which particular accountability forum and for what, could facilitate an empirical assessment of multi-level accountability.

The third layer introduces two analytical perspectives by means of which accountability can be mapped empirically. This section discusses principal–agent analysis as well as constitutional analysis. Taken together, these three sections build towards an analytical framework by which accountability can be mapped and gauged in a multi-level context, which is featured in the fourth section.

The concept of accountability

Defining accountability

Although the term 'accountability' certainly has an intuitive meaning, it proves remarkably hard to define. The body of literature on accountability in general sets out to define the meaning of the term, to provide different typologies and styles of accountability, or discusses its relevance for the functioning of a democratic system of government (e.g. Behn, 2001; Mulgan, 2003; Bovens, 2007a, b; Black, 2008). In parallel, game-theoretical work points towards several mechanisms that underlie the functioning of an accountability arrangement (cf. Lupia, 2000; Strøm, 2000, 2006).

There is a paucity of behavioural research into the workings of accountability (Brandsma, 2013). This may well have to do with the fact that common or unchallenged definitions are lacking. In an analysis on meanings of accountability used in the literature, Bovens (2010, 948–54) concludes that this concept can have two qualitatively different meanings. On the one hand, accountability may be regarded as a virtue, as a property of individuals or institutions that is associated with concepts such as responsiveness or transparency (cf. Koppell, 2005). On the other hand, accountability may be viewed as a mechanism, by which actors are held to account by forums, to whom they are obliged to explain and justify their conduct. The forum can ask questions, pass judgement and impose consequences on the actor. Thus viewed, accountability is not an end in itself, but is functional for specific relationships between institutions or individuals.

Many authors who are interested in accountability as a mechanism (see Bundt, 2000; Page, 2006) take the definition that was developed by Romzek and Dubnick (1987, 228) as a starting point. They define accountability as 'the means by which public agencies and their workers manage the diverse expectations generated within and outside the organization', and they distinguish between four partially overlapping types of accountability: bureaucratic, legal, professional and political accountability. Accountability is not seen as an individual attribute but rather as a means of connecting public agents to a variety of audiences. Similarly, other widely cited definitions of accountability as a mechanism are also relational, and they typically include obligations to explain and justify past conduct to a significant other (Day and Klein, 1987, p. 5; Romzek and Dubnick, 1998, p. 6; Mulgan, 2003, p. 9; Strøm, 2000; Bovens 2007a, b). Depending on the specific type of accountability included in the research, this could refer either to relationships between agents and principals (e.g. Strøm, 2000), between actors and forums (Bovens, 2007a, b) or accountors and accountees (Pollitt, 2003, p. 89).

The concept of accountability as a mechanism is at the centre of the debates about the accountability of comitology. For instance, Schäfer (2000, p. 23) states that 'the awareness on the part of the representatives, both from the Community and the Member State level, that they may be held directly accountable for their decisions would be likely to affect their actions', and Larsson (2003b, p. 157, 169–70) questions whether we now have 'civil servants who are the politician's masters' as opposed to 'civil servants being accountable to elected politicians'. The most widely used definition of accountability as a mechanism in the domain of multi-level governance is that of Bovens (2007b), who defines it as 'a relationship between an actor and a forum, in which the actor has an obligation to explain and justify his or her conduct; the forum can pose questions and pass judgment, and the actor may face consequences'. The present study makes use of this definition of accountability. Other definitions of accountability as a mechanism include similar elements (Day and Klein, 1987, p. 5; Mulgan, 2003, p. 9; Strøm, 2000).

This definition of accountability as a mechanism, including Bovens' definition, can be operationalized according to three elements

(Brandsma and Schillemans, 2013). First comes the provision of *information* by the actor towards the accountability forum. At this stage, the forum is made aware of the behaviour of the actor. In the *discussion* phase, the forum may ask follow-up questions, or the forum and the actor may exchange divergent points of view. This is followed by the final phase of accountability in which the forum makes an *assessment* and decides whether or not to impose *consequences* on the actor. Such consequences may be formal or informal sanctions, but they may equally well be rewards (Mulgan, 2003; Bovens 2007a, b).

The relevance of accountability mechanisms

In modern democracies, the relational interpretation of accountability increases in significance due to the decrease of partisanship in society and the gradual process by which certain parts of policymaking are moving out of the political domain. This decline in partisanship is associated with a decrease in the relevance of party ideology and representation of particular segments in society at the polling booth. As the number of swing voters increases, parties compete more on the basis of issues rather than on ideology, and prospective voting becomes more and more difficult for voters. At the same time, the outsourcing of regulatory competences towards semi-independent, non-majoritarian institutions also challenges the capacity of voters to pursue policy preferences through their votes.

The capacity of citizens to achieve policy outcomes through their votes is even lower in the area of European decision-making, because the European Parliament (and also national parliaments indirectly via governments in the Council of Ministers) only has a weak right of initiative. Furthermore, members of the European Parliament are elected on a national basis rather than on a European one, and election campaigns use separate programmes made by national parties. Once elected, these national parties collaborate in European factions, which show increasing patterns of party discipline (Hix, Noury and Roland, 2005).

Also, the European Parliament does not support the Commission on the basis of a permanent majority coalition, but works on the basis of majorities per issue. On this particular element the EU system is more similar to a presidential system, where the executive does not depend on the support of a legislative majority coalition for survival. On the one hand, this enables more parties to translate their ideas into policies than in systems with coalition governments, but on the other hand, it does make political competition less visible to the general public. And finally, the Council of Ministers represents the member states through its executives rather than through its legislators, which at best can only count on the support of a majority of domestic voters. Prospective voting, thus, is even more difficult with respect to European policymaking than it is for decision-making that neatly fits within the borders of a member state's jurisdiction.

The result is that prospective voting, by necessity, has to give way to retrospective voting: being able to throw the rascals out, and hoping rather than expecting that things will take a turn for the better during the next term (Curtin, Mair and Papadopoulos, 2010, 930; Palumbo, 2010, p. xi). While perhaps not intrinsically is 'one of those golden concepts that no one can be against' in all situations (Bovens, 't Hart and Schillemans, 2008, 225), accountability may thus well be the best we have in order to safeguard popular control and prevent tyranny of government, especially with a view to European governance. This significantly underscores the salience of accountability, given that it helps to control unelected decision-makers – provided the actors indeed face consequences for their behaviour.

Accountability mechanisms can help fulfil a number of aims, all of which also serve as benchmarks for assessing its functioning. Depending on the (normative) aims in scope, different accountability forums may be the focus of empirical research (Bovens, 2007b; Brandsma, 2013). The two most important aims of accountability are to provide for *popular control* and for *checks and balances* (Palumbo, 2010, p. xii–xiv; Przeworski Stokes and Manin, 1999; Strøm, 2000; Bovens, 2007b; Curtin, 2007). In the *popular control* perspective, the primary aim is to have the people's preferences translated into policy, or, to reverse the argument, to avoid the pursuit of policies that run counter to the people's intentions. Information, discussion and the possibility of imposing positive or negative consequences are all meant for checking to what degree policies are in conformity with the constituents' preferences. Accountability, thus, provides feedback to citizens who are able to use this feedback to decide their vote (Strøm, 2000; Bovens, 2007b; Bovens, 't Hart and Schillemans, 2008).

On a slightly different note, a *checks and balances* perspective on accountability argues that there is a need to prevent society from being tyrannized by one government institution or by government as a whole. As a result, it emphasizes the need for independent legality checks by an independent court, and the organization of countervailing powers within clearly defined processes of policymaking. This way society is less at risk of being subject to the will of particular actors within government. In this perspective, accountability serves as one of several possible tools to provide for checks and balances. The formal need for explanation and justification of conduct by an actor to a forum, and the possibility of consequences being imposed by the forum upon the actor, may well create mutual dependencies between different institutions within the same decision-making system. In contrast to the popular control perspective, forums do not necessarily need to connect decision-making institutions to citizens. Ultimately, in the checks and balances perspective, accountability is regarded as a means to maintain the purity of government, which is defined as avoiding the misuse of power (Bovens, 2007b; Curtin, 2007; Bovens, 't Hart and Schillemans, 2008). With respect to accountability for policies, the consequences that forums may impose on actors are to be interpreted as a means to achieve a balanced output. When referring to choices made in the context of designing decision-making processes, choices that are made with respect to organizing accountability are to be interpreted as a means to redress a balance of powers between institutions.

Accountability in multi-level settings

Accountability is therefore key to the functioning of democratic government, even in the absence of prospective voting, whether from a popular control or from a checks and balances perspective. Nevertheless, accountable governance or even accountable government is particularly hard to achieve in systems composed of multiple levels of government, each bounded by their own constituencies but still making decisions in collaborative settings. The question as to what degree multi-level governance is accountable is essentially an empirical one (Bovens, Curtin and 't Hart, 2010). But before actual empirical stocktaking can commence, it must first be specified who is to be held to account, and for what.

Identifying actors and objects of accountability is a more complex endeavour in multi-level governance settings than in more traditional settings. Existing research in this field mainly addresses this matter in conceptual or in theoretical terms, and all in all it presents a deadlock. The debate centres around three complexities of accountability, particularly due to the involvement of multiple levels of government. The conclusion appears to be that there must be a deficit if only for theoretical reasons: the debate presents an impossibility thesis. However, even though the literature rightly points out the complexities involved with the dispersion of actors and forums within even single multi-level governance arrangements, conclusions relating to accountability deficits still primarily build on the assumption that individual actors are supposed to be responsible for the entire decision-making process, even when they have been involved only to a limited degree.

This section dissects the arguments behind the impossibility thesis and shows that actors and forums need to be identified exhaustively, as does the object of accountability for all respective actors and forums. This mapping of actors, forums and objects will allow the discussion to move beyond the impossibility thesis.

The impossibility thesis revisited: Three arguments against multi-level accountability

To begin with the least complicated of the four arguments, there is a compelling normative point that *individual actors cannot justifiably be held to account for the content of a collective decision* (Thompson, 1980). It is, however, a condition *sine qua non* in multi-level governance settings that national authorities are not able to autonomously control decision-making that includes a supranational component (Strøm, Müller and Bergman, 2003, p. 744). Intergovernmental agreements typically succeed or fail as a result of the conduct of any single individual party, as all of the parties involved are effectively veto players. However, the Council of Ministers in the European Union usually employs majority decision-making, as do other collaborative settings where the voting parties include national actors, including comitology. Even unanimous decisions taken under majority voting rules may, and in fact do, obscure minority positions of outvoted governments because of support given in exchange for support on other files (Heisenberg, 2005, 69–70). Individual actors are thus not in full control of the eventual outcome, because different jurisdictions are simultaneously at play in crafting the eventual decision. Hence it has been concluded that the delegation of policies to the European Union has not only stretched the lines of accountability, but also blurred them (Agné, 2009, p. 55; Palumbo, 2010, xii). Without unanimity rules, individual actors cannot be held accountable for the output of the decision-making process: collective decisions.

A second argument that is commonly referred to is that multi-level governance tends to involve *different and more actors than those traditionally conceived of* in international decision-making, and that these actors are able to evade accountability. National authorities increasingly form networks with other national authorities and their international counterparts, bypassing traditional diplomatic circles such as the Foreign Office. Keohane and Nye (1977) call this complex interdependence, and such networks are mushrooming in the European Union. Besides comitology, a multitude of multi-level governance networks are at play, such as networks of regulators (Eberlein and Grande, 2005; Coen and Thatcher, 2008), expert groups (Larsson, 2003a; Gornitzka and Sverdrup, 2011), open method of coordination networks (Borrás and Jacobsson, 2004) or the management boards of supranational agencies (Flinders, 2004). Complex interdependence supposedly facilitates actors to conceal their behaviour and act against the preferences of their constituencies, making use of the obscurity of the networks in which the decisions are usually made (Papadopoulos, 2010, 1039), far away from the prying eyes of the Foreign Office, which regards certain issues to be too low politics or as falling outside their realm of competence. Mostly, network governance takes place behind closed doors or deals with very specialized matters, so that outsiders know very little about the goings on in these networks (Brandsma, Curtin and Meijer, 2008). Also, when diplomatic and specialist lines of delegation are at work at the same time, both covering different aspects of the collective decision-making process, coordination problems may arise (Alfé, Brandsma and Christiansen, 2009, p. 141–2). Taken together, these structural features of complex interdependence are said to encourage ex-post blame shifting and a dilution of responsibilities in multi-level governance settings (Oliver, 2009, p. 13–14; Papadopoulos, 2010, 1033–4). Thus, the multitude of actors as such is said to hinder accountability.

A third issue relates to the *very high number of possible forums*. The rational choice literature argues that simple delegation settings – that is, involving only one forum per actor – deliver more and better accountability, as forums can claim exclusive credit for overseeing an actor (Strøm, 2000, 278). But the European governance system, even disregarding the fact that it consists of multiple levels, is anything but a simple system. Many actors in the European system have multiple principals, and each principal tries to mould the set-up of systems that control the behaviour of actors to its own exclusive needs (Kelemen, 2002; Dehousse, 2008). Also, European policymaking cuts through the traditional *trias politica* in the sense that executive and legislative competences do not neatly coincide with the borders of the institutions, and sometimes the same individuals hold different roles while acting for different institutional actors (Verhey and Claes, 2008, p. 7). And this is only the European side of the picture; the complexity further increases when multi-level characteristics are taken into account with different actors and forums at the member state or even sub-state level. All in all, this not only amounts to a myriad of actors but also to a patchwork of accountability forums, all having different agendas and powers (Vaubel, 2006; Papadopoulos, 2010, 1039).

Competition between forums and different cultures in which those forums are embedded may hinder accountability, in the sense that the object for which account is rendered may become a toy in a different political game than that regarding which account is to be rendered. In the debate about national parliamentary control over European decision-making, for instance, it has been noted that traditional party-political and coalition dynamics always play a major role when ministers are called to account, so that the issue for which account is rendered loses relevance (Peters, 2009, p. 40–1). In a nutshell, the vast number of forums negatively impacts upon the quality of accountability processes.

The 'too many forums' argument, however, has been challenged. Scott, for instance, notes that the multitude of forums may promote rather than hamper accountability; it may bring about *redundancy* (Scott, 2000, 54). In relation to network structures of governance, redundancy includes the existence of multiple accountability forums even across different jurisdictions, each of which are able to monitor the behaviour of particular actors within the network. The individual accountability forums may then serve as 'fire alarms' to one another, so that other forums may pick up signals and closely scrutinize different parts of the broader issue. Redundancy, thus, means that multiple accountability relationships are at work at the same time and that forums cooperate, so that in the end the entire arrangement is controlled. On that note, the plethora of different forums may in fact be an asset rather than a nuisance. Although the notion of control through multiple forums runs counter to the previously presented idea of stronger accountability through fewer forums (Strøm, 2000, 278), the idea that teamwork leads to higher detection chances is not without merit.

It follows logically from this reasoning that a multi-level structure of governance may well increase accountability rather than reduce it: multi-level governance naturally brings about redundancy in the existing accountability arrangements (Scott, 2000, 54). In a similar vein, Mulgan (2003, p. 220) argues that accountability is 'compounded' when every actor involved is held to account by at least one forum. Expanding on this notion, an increase in redundancy – and hence an increase in the number of forums – is thought to naturally constrain the actor, as this will make the behaviour of the individual forums more unpredictable to the actor (Papadopoulos, 2010, 1041).

However, this requires the different forums to oversee the same type of behaviour, if possible also with respect to the very same actors, as they otherwise cannot make effective use of each other's information. Redundant accountability therefore only seems viable in the context of a very specific type of multi-level governance, namely the type where various actors work together in implementing a policy that has already been decided upon at the European level. Financial accountability for European subsidies spent by member states can certainly be redundant accountability, as the object of accountability remains the same across states and jurisdictions. However, redundant accountability for decision-making is simply impossible in a multi-level governance setting, since all member states and EU institutions provide different inputs. While it may certainly be possible to opt for some sort of accountability at the European level for the content of the decision that has been made, it is not possible to do so at the national level, because the actors can justifiably point out that they were in a minority position, or that the eventual output was the only possible compromise. The object of accountability with respect to decision-making therefore changes from outputs to inputs when it crosses the jurisdictional boundary from the European to the member state level. This makes information collected by national accountability forums useless to other national and European forums, and vice versa. More networking of forums (Slaughter, 2005, p. 47–9), therefore, is not the answer in all situations of networked governance (Van de Steeg, 2009).

Breaking the deadlock: Moving beyond the impossibility thesis

The dominant discourse in studies of multi-level accountability points to its impossibility based on the aforementioned theoretical obstacles: there are no unanimity rules, there are many actors, and there are many forums. However, it is still possible, and in fact necessary, to gauge and evaluate accountability empirically. In fact, the two latter arguments do not stand in the way of empirical research. The main theoretical deadlock is the first argument and is of a normative nature: individual actors cannot be individually held to account for the content of a collective decision if unanimity rules are lacking.

The key to breaking the deadlock is taking this as a given rather than as an impediment. Following Slaughter (2005, 62–4), I propose to treat accountability as an individual attribute insofar as behaviour is concerned. For networked decision-making, this means that individuals only need to be able to answer for their own behaviour, even when they represent institutions. In scholarly discussions on accountability, often the accountability of organizations, systems, individuals and positions are mixed together or referred to interchangeably (Page, 2010, 1011). When the object of accountability only refers to the contribution made by each individual actor within an organization, the accountability of each and every actor can be scrutinized. This view is fully compatible with standard conceptions of state sovereignty and network governance. Even when subscribing to the view that primary power rests in the hands of national governments, and thus regarding officials participating in networks as representing the national state – as they formally do – it is still possible to assess the accountability of individuals within a state for their own respective behaviour. Hence the accountability of a multi-level governance setting should be seen as the sum of micro-level accountabilities, and be researched as such. In addition, accountability for individual input also allows different forums to adopt their own respective standards as to the behaviour that is expected from the actors.

In an empirical sense, this approach overcomes all difficulties commonly associated with accountability for multi-level governance settings. Issues relating to the plethora of actors and forums can be investigated by researching specific actor–forum relationships within the multi-level governance arrangement, whether they are supranational or national actors or forums. The challenge is mostly a practical one: often so many actors and forums participate in multi-level decision-making that identifying and investigating them all defies the best of efforts. However, it is the most accurate point of departure if accountability practices are to be gauged empirically.

Analysing accountability

Thus accountability is shown to be both particularly relevant to multi-level governance settings, and at the same time particularly difficult to grasp or analyse in that context. The bulk of the literature in this area identifies theoretical and conceptual reasons explaining why multi-level governance is unlikely to be accountable at all, but very little systematic empirical research has been performed in this area. Existing empirical research in the field consistently addresses only one of the multiple levels involved per arrangement, thereby losing sight of a major set of accountability relationships included in these (Scott and Trubek, 2002; Auel, 2007; Bovens, Curtin and 't Hart, 2010; Brandsma, 2010a; Peers and Costa, 2012). But how to establish to what degree, and where, accountability arises?

Some innovative solutions have been proposed to overcome challenges of multi-level accountability, but these have not yet been embedded into methods of analysis that allow actual practices of accountability to be examined in the light of the two main perspectives of accountability set out before. Before presenting an integrated framework for analysis, let us first examine two analytical strands of research that fit the popular control and checks and balances perspectives of accountability in order to demonstrate what type of analysis is needed in an eventual multi-level framework for analysing accountability. Earlier sections already identified the core ingredients of such a multi-level framework. Accountability is about a relationship between actors and forums, in which the actor informs the forum and the forum may engage in debate with the actor, assess his behaviour and impose consequences (Bovens, 2007b). The type of behaviour at issue reflects the individual contribution of the actor towards the decision-making process (Slaughter, 2005). It goes without saying, however, that specific indicators need to be tailored to the exact governance setting that is under investigation. Yet there are also several generic analytical approaches that are valuable for an empirical account of accountability, since they identify more generic types of indicators from which further specifications can be made, as well as a specification of actors and forums.

This section examines two analytical strands of research that fit the popular control and checks and balances perspectives of accountability, in order to demonstrate the kinds of actors, forums and indicators that are included in the eventual multi-level framework.

Popular control perspective: Principal–agent models

A common way of analysing accountability from a popular control perspective is to make use of principal–agent models. These models present a well-known conceptual toolkit for addressing the relationship between those who delegate power (the principals) and those to whom powers are delegated (the agents). Ultimately derived from the domain of business economics (Miller, 2005, 203–6), the principal–agent approach treats all modern representative democracies as 'chains of delegation': voters (principals) delegate powers to their representatives in Parliament (agents), who in turn (acting as principals) delegate the authority to govern to the cabinet (their agent). This chain of delegation runs all the way from voters (the ultimate principals) to civil servants (who, in the context of multi-level governance, are the ultimate agents). Since any democratic political system ultimately rests upon the notion of government by the citizens, delegation from one authority to the other involves a whole series of principal–agent relationships, ultimately safeguarding popular control (Strøm, 2000; Lane, 2005; Miller, 2005; Lupia, 2006; Strøm, 2006; Strøm, Müller and Bergman, 2006).

Accountability mechanisms from a popular control perspective are meant for keeping a popular 'check' upon the behaviour of public officials enjoying discretion in order to make sure that ultimately the preferences of the people are translated into policy. Using the terminology of the principal–agent framework, this means that the principal must gain some control over the behaviour of its agents, as delegation to an agent involves the transferral of some power or task. Therefore, the agent should be accountable to the principal. Thus, the emphasis of accountability in the principal–agent perspective is on the content of decision-making in light of the delegated tasks (Behn, 2001; Bovens, 2007b). Problems emerge if the agent does not act in the interest of the principal (shirking), which is likely if the principals are not able to monitor the behaviour of the agents effectively (Strøm, 2000, 270–1). To find the appropriate accountability forum, one simply needs to look one step backwards in the chain of delegation. For a minister, parliament would be the appropriate forum; for parliament, it would be the citizens; for the civil service, it would be the minister; and for an individual civil servant, it would be his immediate superior. This way, accountability contributes to the translation of the preferences of the public into decision-making at all stages of decision-making. A direct consequence of this line of reasoning is that a chain of delegation (and its corresponding chain of accountability) is only as strong as its weakest link – an issue which can be mitigated when weak links can be bypassed (Lupia and McCubbins, 2000).

Without going into the specifics and pitfalls of applying the principal–agent framework in behavioural research in a general sense (see Brandsma, 2010b, p. 60–7; Delreux, 2011, 45–52; Waterman and Meier, 1998; Miller, 2005), as the previous theoretical discussion of accountability illustrates, the principal–agent approach has its limits when analysing accountability in a multi-level context. Since multi-level decision-making crosses the borders of jurisdictions, and many actors are involved in making decisions, the object of accountability has to change at some point in the chain of delegation. In domestic decision-making, the content of the final decision can be accounted for within a national system. However, in a multi-level system this can, at best, be traced to the intentions of the actors who made the decision. Although a chain of delegation and accountability is clearly present, account can reasonably only be rendered in respect of input given by individual actors (Curtin and Egeberg, 2008, 652), and individual accountability within member states for the contents of the final collective supranational decision has to be given up on by design.

On top of this, European decision-making typically includes multiple principals per agent. While standard principal–agent models aim to detect to what degree agents may act against the principal's preferences ('agency loss'; cf. Lupia, 2000), a common issue in the European scene is preference disagreement between principals. Often, the principals each have their own political agendas and are not in agreement about the assignment of the agent. In this respect, decisions of delegation by European principals are incomplete contracts that require revision more or less on an ongoing basis, with each revision constituting a ceasefire between institutions. It has been noted in this respect that European Union institutions seem more interested in curbing each other's interests rather than in controlling an agent (Dehousse, 2008, 795–6). This makes it hard to parsimoniously evaluate possible agency losses. Nevertheless, an analysis of the chain of delegation, including intersections between multiple chains of delegation where applicable, as well as the degree to which agents inform their principals and can be sanctioned by them, is informative from a popular control perspective on accountability.

Checks and balances perspective: Constitutional analysis

Since the checks and balances perspective on accountability emphasizes the prevention of the tyranny of a majority or the tyranny of one particular institution, the analytic starting point of this approach is to define the formal powers of actors and forums, as opposed to their actual behaviour. By extension, this perspective also includes locating countervailing sources of power. A balance of powers is achieved by mutual dependence between actors, who may interchangeably act as actors or forums depending on the situation, and by independent judgement by a forum that does not belong to the mutually dependent relationship (Kiewit and McCubbins, 1991). The main challenge in a checks and balances approach is to map out these mutual dependencies, and to assess whether the balance of power is tipped in favour of one actor or not. Since power comes in many different political and legal forms, it is notoriously difficult to quantify. Hence this perspective on accountability is mostly confined to legal research and looking at the constitutional fabric of an institution's set-up.

Constitutional analysis can be used to check whether the theoretical impossibility of multi-level accountability, as proposed by many scholars, actually exists, and if so, where the main issues are located. It helps to identify which actors and forums there are, and where countervailing powers are located. In short, constitutional analysis helps to disaggregate a governance system towards its components.

The main point is to locate countervailing powers at the same level as where a particular power is exercised. In other words, accountability for collective decisions should be in place at the European level, while accounting for individual contributions to those decisions should take place at other appropriate levels. The focus, however, is on formal powers. In the cases of agencies and comitology, for instance, primarily European institutional forums have been under consideration; after all, the supranational level is where formal power is exercised (Bradley, 1992; Busuioc, 2009; Hofmann, 2009).

A framework for analysing multi-level accountability

In sum, the third section shows that we have two valuable analytical toolkits for accountability, each of which can be used to analyse to what degree the two objectives of accountability are actually met, but only as long as there is no sharp division of competences between the individual and aggregate levels. In principal–agent models, the concept of accountability for decision-making is consistently applied throughout the chain of delegation, all the way to the bureaucrats acting in multinational networks, which leads to the object of accountability having to shift away from the content of the final decision towards the input given by a single actor. In the constitutional approach, the input of lower-level participants tends to move out of focus where the formal powers rest at the supranational level, even when these lower-level participants have clearly set their stamp on the final decision.

For analysing the accountability of multi-level governance settings, a more sophisticated framework of analysis is needed that incorporates the multi-level nature of decision-making into its core. In principle, following Scott (2000, 41), the key to understanding a system of accountabilities is to disentangle accountability into the following question: who (i.e. what actor) is held to account by whom (i.e. what forum), and about what? Clearly, it is the latter part of the question that has proven to be the crucial aspect so far.

Figure 3.1 presents a framework for analysing multi-level accountability that addresses this matter in all its complexity, with its application to the comitology case put in brackets. It takes due account of all involved actors at different levels of decision-making, including their forums.

By distinguishing between accountability for collective decisions and accountability for individual input, this framework overcomes the difficulty in applying traditional notions of accountability. Moreover, it allows for both principal–agent inspired, as well as constitutionally inspired, analysis. For instance, both types of delegation settings are included in the framework: from national authorities towards national

Accountability and Multi-Level Governance   59

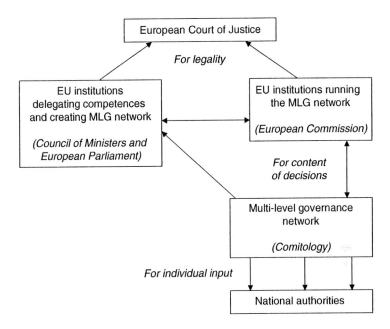

Figure 3.1 Multi-level accountability

participants in the networks, as well as from the European institutions towards other institutions, while in the meantime setting up an instrumental network in that relationship. Accordingly, at the institutional level, checks and balances can be observed between different institutions, including the role of networks themselves in balancing the power of institutions, as well as independent judicial review.

Also, the three levels of analysis identified in Chapter 1 become apparent in this framework of multi-level accountability. The *system level* addresses the make-up of the system that is put in place, probing which of the arrows plotted in Figure 3.1 are actually in place, and how these are supposed to operate in a formal sense. Which actor–forum relationships are specified in the system's set-up? Which specific requirements for transmitting information and discussion exist in each of these relationships, and what consequences can the forum impose on the actor?

The *committee level* concerns the actual functioning of those arrangements with respect to actors operating at the European level. To what degree is information actually transmitted and processed; do discussions take place; and are assessments made (and eventually consequences imposed)?

Finally, the *participant level* addresses the same questions, but with respect to individual actors operating at levels below the European level. For comitology, this concerns the individual input given by each national participant vis-à-vis forums within their own respective jurisdictions.

Let us move back at this point to the essence of accountability. It was argued at the beginning of this chapter that the main two reasons why accountability is deemed relevant are that it serves to guarantee popular control and thwart tyranny by putting into place a balance of power through mutual dependence. On the basis of the framework of multi-level accountability presented here, both these ultimate aims of accountability can be researched through analysis inspired both by principal–agent models and constitutional analysis, thus to arrive at a full picture of the workings of a multi-level accountability regime.

The key normative benchmarks for evaluating the set-up and functioning of accountability, of course, are different in the sense that the objectives of the two perspectives differ. For the popular control perspective the questions run parallel to lines of delegation. Does the design of an accountability arrangement allow for principals to control decision-making delegated to an agent? To what degree does the accountability system put in place information obligations towards hierarchically superior forums, and to what degree can they step in? On a more operational note, how does the formal structure play out in practice? And with respect to the participants in the multi-level governance network, to what degree are their national superiors effectively informed of the contribution they make to collective decision-making?

The checks and balances perspective addresses the countervailing powers that are embedded in the system. As several court cases have demonstrated over the past decades (Türk, 2000; Dehousse, 2003; Bradley, 2006; Peers and Costa, 2012), the Court is able to rule on the legality of comitology decision-making. Hence, the main outstanding questions are which mutual dependencies between the European institutions have been put in place through comitology, as well as which dependencies exist between the institutions and comitology as such. Much as this involves system-level choices, it also plays out in the actual interaction patterns between the Commission and the committee participants. Given that the committee participants are seen as actors balancing the Commission due to their formal capacity of being member state representatives, this also presupposes some degree of accountability of individual committee participants within their respective member states, in order to ensure that the input given by them indeed reflects a national position.

Conclusion: Three levels, two perspectives

This chapter has put forward a framework that enables research into accountability in multi-level settings. The framework goes beyond providing definitions or typologies of accountability, an abundance of which has been provided in the literature over the past decades. Most importantly, it comes to terms with the multi-level characteristics embedded in most of the current 'new' governance arrangements. Multi-level governance involves a fusion of different actors of different kinds, from different jurisdictions. This necessarily implies the presence of a variety of accountability forums – all with competence for part of the governance arrangement. Notions of accountability, apart from only a handful of exceptions, are applied to this type of governance setting in a rather unitary fashion, thereby ignoring the very nature of multi-level governance. Insofar as structural complexities are recognized, authors tend to be pessimistic in the face of the challenges presented by the multi-level structure; yet standard, unitary notions of accountability simply cannot be applied.

The framework presented here incorporates the structural features of different overlapping jurisdictions, thereby taking a first step towards systematic empirical research into accountability for multi-level governance settings. The empirical chapters of this book explore different aspects of the scheme presented in this chapter, which, in the end, adds up to the full picture of accountability at all levels included in the multi-level governance setting of comitology. Chapter 4 pays specific attention to the design of the comitology system, thereby addressing both mutual dependencies and accountability relationships following lines of delegation. Based on an analysis of the process of the coming into existence of the comitology regime following the entry into force of the Lisbon Treaty, the chapter explains the intentions and aims of the actors involved in the design of the system.

Chapter 5 moves down one level of analysis to that of the committees themselves for a discussion of their accountability towards the European institutions. It elucidates both the behaviour of the European Parliament with respect to the information it receives on comitology decision-making on a day-to-day basis, as well as the interaction patterns between committee members and the European Commission that exemplify their mutual dependence in the operation of comitology. The key issues in this chapter are what comitology's accountability regime offers in practice with respect to checks and balances, and the degree to which it is subject to popular control. Chapter 6, as the final empirical chapter, investigates accountability at the level of individual participants. It addresses the interaction between the committee participants and the Commission in terms of the balancing potential of comitology vis-à-vis the Commission, as well as accountability at the national level from committee participants to their superiors for their contribution to the collective decision-making in comitology.

4
System-Level Accountability: Conflict Over Control

Introduction

Comitology is conventionally seen as an instrument through which the member states and the Council can hold the Commission accountable. But comitology also acts as a decision-maker in its own right, which begs the question: how is comitology itself held to account? Ever since the first comitology committees were set up, the system of delegating powers to the Commission while controlling these via committees of member state representatives has been controversial and the subject of bitter interinstitutional conflicts. Essentially, these were and still are about accountability, both from a popular control as well as from a checks and balances perspective. When the legislators delegate powers to the Commission, how do they envisage these powers being controlled through comitology? And how do the institutions balance one another's powers through the set-up of the committee system?

This first of three empirical chapters on the multi-level accountability of comitology focuses exclusively on the design of the comitology system. Addressing accountability at the *system level* of comitology, this chapter runs through 50 years of system design. Which actor–forum relationships does the system include, and what requirements as to information, discussion and consequences are specified for each of these relationships?

This chapter is divided into two sections. The first provides a historical overview of the development of the comitology system, from the installation of the first committee in the early 1960s up until a major reform that was carried out between 2009 and 2011. It illustrates which accountability relationships were constructed and which were not. These 50 years of history are essential for understanding the motives that led to the establishment of the present accountability arrangement.

This was put in place following the entry into force of the Lisbon Treaty, which provided a landmark opportunity for all institutions to completely redesign the committee system, if necessary even from scratch.

This is why the second section of this chapter presents a case study of this reform. It reconstructs the entire inter-institutional decision-making process and, on the basis of formal and informal documents, traces the moves and countermoves of all the relevant actors. What structures – in terms of information, discussion and possibilities for imposing consequences – did the negotiators envisage; and, in the end, which of these actually materialized? The course of events shows how the seemingly simple question of designing an accountability system provoked battles within and between institutions, which resulted in an extraordinarily complicated set of agreements that, beyond doubt, poses a challenge to every practitioner having to work with these agreements on a daily basis.

The design of the comitology system: Fifty years of trench warfare

The origin of the comitology system dates back to 1962. That year, after three years of negotiations between the (brand new) European Commission and the Council of Ministers, the first piece of Community legislation was passed in the process of establishing a common agricultural market. It required the European authorities to manage this market continuously, and the means by which the Commission would be controlled by the member states proved to be one of the main controversies in the negotiations. According to Article 155 of the Treaty of Rome, the Commission was to exercise implementing powers delegated to it by the Council, but this Article did not mention whether the Council could impose conditions on the Commission regarding how to exercise these powers.

The Netherlands categorically rejected any form of intergovernmental control over the Commission, while Germany demanded that the Council, rather than the Commission have the final word. France insisted on decision-making committees, as opposed to the consultative ones that had been introduced in the field of competition shortly before (Bergström, 2005, p. 48–52).

Deadlock was broken by the Commission, which made a compromise proposal that was acceptable to all member states. This solution included the setting up of a management committee of member state administrators having the power to vote by qualified majority on draft-implementing measures proposed by the Commission. The Commission was allowed to adopt its implementing measure regardless of the opinion of the committee, but if the committee voted against the draft-implementing act, the Council was empowered to take a different decision within one month. This solution gave the Commission more or less a free hand in implementing the common agricultural policy, with the Council only entering the picture in the case of particularly controversial measures. At the same time, the arrangement allowed the member states to continuously influence the Commission (Bergström, 2005, p. 52–3, Blom-Hansen, 2008). Thus, the first committee was born whose opinions produced binding effects, and this procedure served as a template for committee procedures introduced in further basic legislation (Haibach, 2000, p. 186–7). Under this system, the Commission became the actor, while the management committee served as a permanent forum and the Council as a forum for appeal against negative consequences. The Commission informed the committee of its intentions and discussed draft executive measures, after which the committee took a vote. This can be seen as a two-step approach to consequences in this accountability system: the committee voted; and, depending on the outcome, the Council could (but did not have to) take a different decision.

This innovative solution meant that comitology was added to the set of accountability and control mechanisms that already existed at that time. Other possibilities were simply not to delegate implementing powers to the Commission in basic legislation, or to answer Parliamentary questions, or to curtail the Commission by means of procedural requirements of consultation and reporting on this. The main innovation of comitology was that member state representatives could delegate issues to the Commission while still permanently overseeing their implementation, without increasing the Council's own workload.

Controversies over the accountability of the comitology system flared up right from the start (Bradley, 1997, 231–5). The European Parliament suspected that the system of management committees allowed the Commission and the member states to sneak politically significant decisions into implementing measures, thereby bypassing consultation of the European Parliament under the normal legislative procedures of that day and age. Also, the European Parliament had not been involved in the designing of the committee system, and it feared that its role as an accountability forum towards the Commission would be hollowed out. After all, the Commission was now primarily placed under the control of management committees that in turn were not accountable to the European Parliament (Haibach, 2000, p. 188–9; Schäfer, 2000, p. 17). Much to the distress of the European Parliament, the Commission renounced the idea of assuming political responsibility for the work of the committees, as well as of limiting the scope of executive measures (Bergström, 2005, p. 54–7). An inter-institutional conflict over comitology was born, which was to turn into a trench war. Although the powers of the European Parliament with respect to comitology have gradually increased over the course of history, its struggle to become an accountability forum of approximately equal strength as the committees has structured the political battlefield up to the present day.

Generic system choices through codification

In the meantime, backed by a number of Court rulings that allowed it to confer implementing powers on the Commission while controlling these via comitology committees (Türk, 2000, p. 219–20; Bergström, 2005, p. 94–104), the Council made a habit of inserting comitology provisions into new legislation. But depending on the political salience of the issues at hand, variations on the original management committee model were invented (Schäfer, 2000, p. 16). Some required an explicit positive vote in the committee before the Commission could go ahead and adopt its measures; others provided the Council with the means to block the adoption of a measure by a simple majority after referral. And many more variations were introduced: by the mid-1980s the number of different procedures had grown to over 30, the number of committees had increased to several hundred (Haibach, 2000, p. 187; Schäfer, 2000, p. 17), and negotiations over committee procedures had become lengthier than ever. The Commission then tried to limit such discussions to choosing among several variants on an exhaustive list, and in the Single European Act, even managed to have an article inserted stating that such a list be drafted in the form of a Council act (Bergström, 2005, p. 179–89). This was to become the 1987 Comitology Decision (Council Decision 1987/373/EEC), which specified five different committee procedures, plus two additional procedures that allowed individual member states to refer external trade safeguard measures to the Council without necessarily having to convene a committee. Table 4.1 lists the five committee procedures, and sets out the consequences that the committees could impose: their and the Council's blocking power over executive measures. The procedures are ordered by the strength of the possible consequences.

Hence the 1987 Comitology Decision still exclusively treats the Commission as the actor and the committees and the Council as forums.

Table 4.1 Committee powers defined in the 1987 Comitology Decision

Procedure	Committee stage	Appeal stage (Council of Ministers)
Advisory	No binding consequences	No appeal
Management, variant a	If qualified majority against: – referral to Council – Commission always adopts its measure but is free to suspend its application for one month pending consideration by the Council	Council has one month to take a different decision by qualified majority
Management, variant b	If qualified majority against: – referral to Council – Application of measure suspended pending consideration by the Council	Council has three months to take a different decision by qualified majority
Regulatory, variant a	If no qualified majority in favour: – referral to Council – Commission cannot adopt measure	Council has three months to take a different decision by qualified majority, otherwise Commission adopts measure
Regulatory, variant b	If no qualified majority in favour: – referral to Council – Commission cannot adopt measure	Council can block adoption by simple majority and may take a different decision within three months by qualified majority
Other	Acts adopted before entry into force of 1987 Decision: see basic act	

Source: Council Decision 1987/373/EEC.

Interestingly, the Council insisted in its Decision that the old, individually negotiated committee provisions in basic acts would not be aligned to the new system. The new, exhaustive list of procedures could ease discussions about the establishment of new committees, but by no means did this result in a thinning out of the jungle of procedures that already existed.

The management and regulatory committee types sought to establish member state control, or, perhaps more accurately, Council control, over the Commission. Since at that time the Council was the only European legislator, this arrangement can easily be understood from a popular control perspective. The Council delegated powers, and it preferred to control the powers it delegated. From the checks and balances point of view, comitology rendered the member states and the Commission mutually dependent: the Commission could formally propose executive measures, while the member states could impose consequences with binding effects. The strength of this relationship was determined by the strength of the voting procedure.

Three accountability issues, however, remained unresolved. The first was that the system was premised on the assumption that the member state civil servants staffing the committees acted upon the same preferences as the Council would do. As we will see later in Chapters 5 and 6, in practice this is not always the case. The diplomats working in the Council sometimes have different considerations than the technical experts sent to the comitology committees (Alfé, Brandsma and Christiansen, 2009, p. 141–2). The Council thus accepts the relinquishment of some decision-making power, precisely because of comitology. A second issue was that the European Parliament, under the consultation procedure, was consulted on the proposed new legislation before the Council legislated. A similar consultation procedure was lacking when implementing measures were referred to the Council.

Third, and most important, was and is that the definition of who the actor is in this arrangement may well be different from how the system is formally laid down. Through their mutual dependency in the committees, the Commission and the member states effectively create implementing measures together; thereby creating a multi-level system of decision-making at the European level that is beyond the control of the European Parliament. After all, one of the main tasks of the European Parliament is to oversee the Commission – that is, the Commission only. To some extent, comitology might be regarded as adding extra checks and balances, with the Council balancing the European Parliament's powers of scrutiny over the Commission through the use of committees. However, effective veto powers over individual policy measures cannot compare to a generic right to ask questions to the Commission and to send it home in its entirety. The Parliament, therefore, felt that comitology distorted the relationship between the Commission and Parliament, and undermined the system of checks and balances specified in the Treaty (Haibach, 2000, p. 190; Bradley, 1997). The Commission's refusal to accept political responsibility for the work of the committees only contributed to this interpretation (Bergström, 2005, p. 54–7).

It was mainly for this reason that the European Parliament continued its fight against power that could be exercised through the comitology system (Haibach, 2000, p. 191). When consulted in the run-up to the adoption of the 1987 Decision, the Parliament demanded, in debates

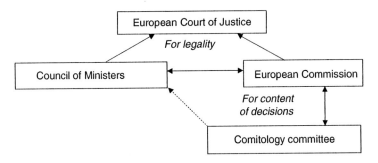

Figure 4.1 Accountability in the pre-Maastricht comitology system

with the Commission as well as through amendments, that the regulatory procedure be abolished and preferably the advisory procedure be applied; that the European Parliament be consulted when matters were referred to the Council; and that it be informed of all draft measures sent to the committees. These demands were all ignored by the Commission, which believed that these would not be acceptable to the Council in the first place. This led the Parliament to block the legislative process, which it did by not formally delivering its opinion. In the end, the Parliament's attempts failed: when the Commission finally gave in and the Parliament formally gave its opinion, all the Parliament's amendments were resoundingly rejected by the Council, which instead even added extra restrictive procedures. Displeased with this result, the European Parliament took a very activist stance against any regulatory procedure proposed in new legislation for the decade to come (Bergström, 2005, p. 192–204; Héritier et al., 2012, p. 36). The Commission, too, decided never to propose the b-variant of the regulatory committee in any of its legislative proposals. The Council nonetheless established no less than 37 such committees in the three years following the entry into force of the 1987 Decision (Schäfer, 2000, p. 18). Inter-institutional rivalry thus continued, with the role of accountability forum at stake. Figure 4.1 shows the accountability structure at the European level, where the full lines represent complete lines of accountability and the dashed line represents an incomplete or partial one.

The rise of the European Parliament

Up to this point in history, actor–forum relationships and their import for comitology can be discerned with relative ease. However, with the entry into force of the Maastricht Treaty and the introduction of co-decision, the picture became considerably more complicated. The European Parliament became a full lawmaker and had to accept becoming an accomplice in inserting committee provisions into new legislation by choosing from a list of committee procedures drawn up by the Council. Yet the European Parliament was not able to co-decide on the set-up of the comitology system itself, as that issue was excluded from co-decision; and it was not an accountability forum under the existing system (Haibach, 2000, p. 199). In terms of accountability, this amounted to a veritable accountability gap, especially from a popular control perspective.

Tension between the accountability interests of the Council and the European Parliament produced legislative deadlock at first instance: the Council insisted on a regulatory procedure while the Parliament insisted on an advisory procedure (Bradley, 1997, 238–40). The tension was only eased by the conclusion of a series of inter-institutional agreements, which granted the European Parliament rights that were not provided for in the Treaties or in the Comitology Decision. The most notable of these were the Modus Vivendi adopted in December 1994 and the Samland-Williamson agreement of September 1996.

The Modus Vivendi stipulated that the European Parliament was to receive all draft measures discussed in the committees, and that in the event of referral to the Council, it would first seek the opinion of the European Parliament: in other words, it was provided with information on all issues, it could discuss the most controversial ones, but had no opportunities of imposing consequences (Haibach, 2000, p. 201–2). The Samland-Williamson agreement added to this the forwarding of annotated committee agendas in advance of the committee discussions and the results of votes in regulatory and management committees. The agreement also provided that the European Parliament might request access to committee meetings, but since such requests were to be decided by unanimity in committee and some member states categorically rejected such participation, this part of the agreement proved to be a dead letter (Haibach, 2000, p. 204; Alfé and Christiansen, 2009, p. 59). Despite these efforts, tension over choosing committee procedures in basic legislation persisted. The European Parliament systematically preferred less stringent procedures to more stringent ones, and the Council systematically preferred the opposite (Franchino, 2000a).

In the year 1999, the comitology system was reformed, again using the consultation procedure. The European Parliament made a bid for introducing a parliamentary legality check, in exchange for accepting the regulatory procedure (Bergström, 2005, p. 264). This strategy paid off as it was granted this right, albeit with a very limited scope. The 1999 Comitology Decision (Council Decision 1999/468/EC) gave the European Parliament the power to adopt a non-binding resolution if it considered an implementing act to exceed the scope provided for in the basic legislation upon which the implementing act was based. This power did not add to those of the Court of Justice, but it could be used for 'whistle-blowing' purposes. The accompanying information rights were obtained through an inter-institutional agreement concluded with the Commission shortly thereafter, but this agreement simultaneously limited the time for the European Parliament to adopt such a resolution – in plenary – to one month only.[1]

More or less at the same time, the Court of Justice ruled in a case lodged by tobacco company *Rothmans* that the Commission was responsible for access to document requests on comitology committees,[2] effectively making comitology subject to the same transparency rules as the Commission (Dehousse, 2003). This paved the way for making comitology more transparent. Subsequent efforts to make comitology documents available through an online repository, albeit an incomplete one, facilitated the monitoring capacities of civil society actors who, in turn, were at least potentially enabled to act as 'fire alarms' of the European Parliament (Brandsma, Curtin and Meijer, 2008).

The 1999 Decision also changed the voting rules of the committees and limited the number of procedures to three, plus one special procedure for adopting safeguard measures. Table 4.2 lists their powers over the Commission.

In this, way, the 1999 system reduced the likelihood that the member states could impose consequences on the Commission. The mechanism of rejecting a draft measure in the Council through a simple majority was abolished (but replaced by a non-binding declaration that the Commission was to avoid going against any 'predominant position' that might emerge in the Council) (Haibach, 2000, p. 211). It is also noteworthy that, in contrast to the previous Comitology Decision, a gradual alignment to the new rules of the game was provided for, but only when the relevant legislation was due for update. The Parliament, however, despite its acceptance of the existence of the regulatory procedure, continued to be biased against using this procedure for the delegation of broad powers (Héritier and Moury, 2011). Hence the 1999 reform finally recognized, in a very limited way, the European Parliament's role as an accountability forum, while the member states accepted weaker control powers.

Table 4.2 Committee powers defined in the 1999 and 2006 Comitology Decisions

Procedure	Committee stage	Appeal stage (Council)
Advisory	No binding consequences	No appeal
Management	If qualified majority against: – referral to Council – Commission always adopts its measure but is free to suspend its application for three months pending consideration by the Council	Council has three months to take a different decision by qualified majority
Regulatory	If no qualified majority in favour: – referral to Council – Commission cannot adopt measure	Council has three months to object to the Commission's proposal by qualified majority, otherwise Commission adopts measure
Regulatory with scrutiny (as from 2006)	If qualified majority in favour: – referral to Council and European Parliament – Commission cannot adopt measure	Council and European Parliament both have three months to block adoption, both on limited grounds, the Council using qualified majority voting. If neither blocks, Commission adopts measure
	Otherwise: – referral to Council – Commission cannot adopt measure	Council has two months to block adoption by qualified majority; otherwise European Parliament has four months to block adoption on limited grounds. If European Parliament does not block, Commission adopts measure
Other	Acts adopted before entry into force of 1987 Decision and never aligned to the 1999 system: see basic act for specific procedure	

Source: Council Decisions 1999/468/EC and 2006/512/EC.

Towards constitutional change

The comitology system was slightly modified in the year 2006. This amendment must be seen in the context of the failed Constitutional Treaty, which proposed to single out measures amending or supplementing non-essential elements (i.e. Annexes) in existing legislation from the sphere of implementing measures and to create a new legal category for these: delegated legislation, which was supposed to be jointly controlled by the Council and the European Parliament (Puntscher-Riekmann and Slominski, 2009, 321–8). Because of the failure of the Constitutional Treaty, a limited change was carried out within the existing legal framework to allow for parliamentary control within the comitology system – but only insofar as this concerned comitology measures on adapting annexes to existing co-decision legislation (Héritier et al., 2012, p. 40–6). The 2006 amendment to the 1999 Comitology Decision (Council Decision 2006/512/EC) introduced a new committee procedure for this: the regulatory procedure with scrutiny. It allowed both the Council and the European Parliament to veto a draft measure that exceeded its legal scope, went against the aims of the basic legislation, or failed to respect the principles of subsidiarity or proportionality. In this regard, the opinion of the committee in question was of less relevance: after a positive opinion, both institutions could object within three months, whereas after a negative opinion, first the Council was granted two months in which to object, followed by four months for the European Parliament if the Council had not already objected. Given its wider powers of scrutiny, the European Parliament has been much more willing to choose this procedure when adopting new legislation, and existing legislation has gradually been aligned to the new provisions.

The 1999 system, including the 2006 amendment, remained in force until shortly after the entry into force of the Lisbon Treaty. We have seen thus far in the development of the comitology system that it has become harder for the member states to impose consequences on the Commission, and that new lines of accountability have been added in the course of time. However, each of these new accountability relationships only applies to a subset of cases, making the overall set-up of the accountability regime quite messy. Figure 4.2 again summarizes the set-up

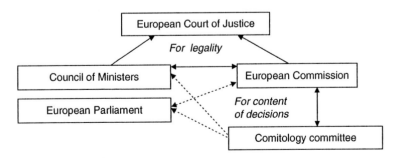

Figure 4.2 Accountability in the 1999/2006 comitology system

at the European level only, and again full lines represent complete lines of accountability and dashed lines represent incomplete or partial ones.

Under this system, the Commission, as the actor, and the member states in the comitology committees balance each other's powers since they are dependent on each other for making decisions. It is through the use of committees that the Council can control the Commission or to some degree balance its powers. But when taking the committees as the actor, no lines of accountability are provided for towards the Council itself, other than that the Council can confirm an already negative committee opinion, or when the regulatory procedure with scrutiny applies. Accountability relationships are therefore lacking for the many situations where the committee decides not to block a proposed Commission measure under the management or regulatory procedures. The European Parliament effectively only plays a role under the regulatory procedure with scrutiny, as its sole other prerogative is sending out non-binding political messages on legality before a very short deadline, and only when it concerns implementing measures based on co-decision legislation.

The Lisbon Treaty presented all institutions with a rare opportunity to clear up this picture, as well as finally to complete it with respect to ensuring popular control and checks and balances. In the same vein as the failed Constitutional Treaty, the Lisbon Treaty makes a distinction between delegated acts with control exercised by the Council and the European Parliament (Article 290 TFEU), and implementing acts with control by the member states (Article 291 TFEU). The modalities of this member state control, however, would not be decided by the Council alone under the consultation procedure, which had hitherto been the case, but rather by means of a regulation adopted by the European Parliament and the Council together. Before the entry into force of the Lisbon Treaty, the European Parliament could only push to increase its powers through political power play (Pollack, 2003a, 120; Franchino, 2007, p. 283; Bradley, 2008, 850; Bergström, Farrell and Héritier, 2007), making the process leading up to the adoption of the new control regime for implementing acts the first opportunity that the European Parliament ever had to actually co-decide on the set-up of the comitology system.

It is therefore worthwhile to take a closer look at the design of the new comitology system, and to see what the intentions of the institutions were when faced with the opportunity to redesign its accountability. As will be shown later on, accountability has been significantly strengthened in some respects while weakened in others, and the resulting regime has become messier than ever before for all sorts of – mainly political – reasons.

Negotiating a new comitology system

Only a few days after the entry into force of the Lisbon Treaty, the institutions formally began working on the design of the new system for delegated and implementing acts. Article 291 (TFEU) specifies that a co-decision Regulation must lay down the rules governing the committee system, while Article 290 (TFEU) requires no further rules to become operative. The latter Article provides that the Council and Parliament can delegate the power to adopt non-legislative acts supplementing or amending non-essential elements of a basic legislative act to the Commission, while the Council and the European Parliament can control this power. The same Article also stipulates that the two legislators may decide to revoke this power or to block the adoption of individual measures through a qualified majority vote in the Council or an absolute majority vote in the European Parliament's plenary, and that control mechanisms are to be defined in each basic piece of legislation.

Article 290 (TFEU) thus clearly identifies the Commission as the actor, and the Council and Parliament as accountability forums. Given that the Commission both initiates new policies (and hence also has to formulate a proposal for control of delegated measures in its initiatives) and is in charge of adopting delegated acts once it receives these powers, it presented its views on how to apply this power in practice through a non-legislative communication. The European Parliament adopted a resolution in response to this communication and pressed for the adoption of an inter-institutional agreement, which finally happened in early 2011.

These were only the formal steps. Informal pre-negotiations had already taken place before the Commission sent its communication and initiative to the Council and the European Parliament. The analysis, therefore, begins in November 2009. As far as delegated acts are concerned, the negotiation process ended when the Commission, the Council and Parliament agreed on the content of a common understanding on 16 December 2010. As to implementing acts, the process ended with the adoption of the 2011 Comitology Regulation on 14 February 2011. In between, several formal points in the decision-making process were passed, and numerous intra- and inter-institutional negotiations took place behind closed doors.

Data

For the purpose of the analysis, use was made of both formal and informal sources. These are listed in the Annex. First, several documents were retrieved that revealed the institutions' positions. Some of these were official documents that could be found in the EU's online document repositories, such as European Parliament reports, COREPER agendas, the Commission's communication and its legislative proposal relating to the two types of acts. In addition, a variety of actors who, in one way or the other, were involved in the negotiations on these files confidentially made large amounts of informal documentation available, such as meeting documents, non-papers and minutes. Second, several of those actors kept me posted about ongoing events. Because some documents were only available to a very select number of actors, at various points in the following analysis document references have been omitted in order not to jeopardize the anonymity of the sources.

The analysis is split into two parts, representing the negotiations on both the delegated and implementing acts systems. The analysis is presented in the form of a detailed chronological narrative, in order to provide a thick description of the actors' moves and countermoves, and to help to understand the very messy accountability structure that has finally been decided upon. Finally, the accountability gains and losses are identified by comparing the current system to previous ones.

Negotiating the accountability of delegated acts

The Commission, the Council and the European Parliament all relied on extensive delegation during the negotiations. On behalf of the Commission, a team was formed by the secretariat-general. In the Council, the issue rotated with the presidency. At the European Parliament, the Legal Affairs committee was put in charge, which appointed Jószef Szájer as its rapporteur on both issues – the same MEP who negotiated the alignment of the acquis to the Regulatory Procedure with Scrutiny in 2006. These negotiators, in turn, were advised by a variety of actors such as actors within member states and services within the institutions.

Delegated acts: The Commission's first move

Although Article 290 (TFEU) does not require any secondary legislation in order to be applied, both the Parliament and Council presidency expressed in the run-up to the entry into force of the Treaty that it would be useful if the three institutions reached an understanding on standard recitals, and on how the Commission would use its delegated powers (Council, 2009a; European Parliament, 2009a). While preparing its Communication of 9 December 2009 on this, the Commission already informally shared its views with the Council and the European Parliament in November 2009 through several non-papers.

These non-papers reveal several initial intentions. First, the Commission stresses that the delegation of power should, as a rule, be infinite, since the legislative power is entitled to revoke delegated powers. It strongly rejects the idea of subjecting the delegation of power to a sunset clause in basic legislation. Second, the Commission stresses that it is free to choose its own work processes in the run-up to adopting a delegated act, but still intends to consult experts from member states through expert groups as a general rule. It thus voluntarily commits to an exchange of information and discussion with member state representatives, but also defends its freedom of procedural choice. But finally, it also aims to limit the Council and Parliament in the consequences these bodies can impose: it proposes some conditions to which legislative oversight should be subject. This includes limiting the means of the Council and Parliament to the revocation of delegated power and/or the right of opposition against individual measures only; a three-month time limit for expressing opposition but also committing to inform the Commission of a possible intention to oppose or revoke within one month; and an urgency procedure for adopting temporary delegated acts without possibility for objection by the Parliament and Council. The Commission also proposes standard wording to be used in new legislation, based on the aforesaid.

Delegated acts: Initial responses from the European Parliament and the Council

In a series of informal bilateral and trilateral meetings in November and December 2009, both the European Parliament and the Council expressed several concerns. The European Parliament primarily objected to the idea that its role as an accountability forum could be subjected to limits, in particular as to the consequences it could impose on the Commission and the timing of doing so. In its eyes, particularly problematic was the fact that urgency acts could be adopted without any scrutiny by the legislators, as well as the proposed time limit of only one month to consider opposing or revoking, after which it would have another two months to finalize its own internal processes. To the Parliament, these deadlines were too short, since such issues have to be discussed and voted upon both at the committee level and in plenary. Also, it considered that delegation should not be infinite by default, since it is up to the legislators to decide this. Finally, the Parliament considered it useful to reach a common understanding on the approach regarding delegated acts only after some experience had been gained with the new procedure.

After the Commission modified its non-paper by making urgency measures subject to control and by not making delegation of powers infinite by default, discussions in the Council's Mertens Group mainly focused on an age-old issue: if and how to delegate its role as an accountability forum to a committee of member state representatives. However, since the Lisbon Treaty formally got rid of committees in the realm of delegated acts, the member states' challenge was to secure consultation of national experts without making the system resemble old-fashioned comitology too much.

Several member states insisted on the following points (Council, 2009b). First, national experts should not only be consulted as a 'general rule' but also systematically. Second, member states sought assurance that consultation of national experts included *all* member states. Third, the expert groups should have sufficient time to give input to the Commission, and finally the Commission must summarize the main elements brought forward in the discussion, together with a preliminary reaction and an indication of the Commission's intentions on the basis of the member state experts' input. In short, the Council sought to ensure that the expert groups would continue to function as an accountability forum to the Commission, albeit without formal capabilities of imposing consequences. Those, of course, could be imposed by the Council, to which the expert groups could signal controversial issues.

The Commission accepted all of this, and moreover agreed to send an explanatory memorandum with each adopted delegated act, providing information about its preparatory work, including the consultation of experts. Furthermore, the Council was of the opinion that a standard revocation or opposition time limit of three months was more appropriate than the proposed one plus two months, and that instances could be envisaged where delegation to the Commission would not be infinite, but not subject to automatic renewal either (Council, 2009b, c).

Delegated acts: The Commission's second move

The Commission's Communication of 9 December 2009 was a second step, following consultation with the legislative institutions. Compared to its earlier non-papers, the Communication still expressed a strong preference for infinite delegation, but it also considered the appropriateness of automatic renewal or expiry dates for delegated powers. It also mentioned the systematic consultation of experts from *all* member states, except – and this is new – in cases where there is no requirement for new expertise. All other points raised by the other institutions were taken on board by the Commission as well (European Commission, 2009b).

Delegated acts: Reactions from the European Parliament

The first confrontation between the institutions took place on an environmental issue. The first new piece of legislation following the Lisbon Treaty in which a delegated act procedure was provided for happened to relate to pet animals (European Parliament and Council Regulation 438/2010/EU). Since a common approach between the institutions had not yet been agreed, this regulation was seen as an important test case. Conflicts between the institutions all centred on accountability: time limits for objection by the legislator (with the Commission favouring short deadlines and the Parliament long ones), duration of delegation and the involvement of national experts (with the Council demanding this and the European Parliament objecting to this).

In trialogues, the three institutions agreed on solutions that set an important precedent. First, the time limits for objection were set to 2 + 2 months. Initially, both the Council and Parliament could take two months to decide whether or not to oppose a delegated act. If neither institution decided to do so, the Commission could adopt the act in question. Otherwise, the Parliament and the Council could spend an additional two months formalizing objections. Second, the duration of delegation was fixed at five years, but made automatically renewable. Third, the Parliament succeeded in removing references to a privileged position for 'national' experts from the preambles, and replacing these with the more neutral wording 'it is of particular importance that the Commission carries out appropriate consultations during its preparatory work, including at expert level'. This, obviously, leaves more room for the Commission. The latter point also shows that the European Parliament was not interested in strong accountability as such. Rather than strengthening its own role as an accountability forum, it sought to limit the role of other accountability forums so as to achieve a balance between forums (European Parliament and Council Regulation 438/2010/EU).

In contrast to the report on implementing powers (see further), only two parliamentary committees expressed their opinion on the Commission's communication on delegated acts to rapporteur Szájer. His final report included several elements that are also found in the case of pet animals. First, the report stressed that the objection period of 2 + 2 months should be seen as a minimum, and that there was no formal role for national experts since they should be consulted in the capacity of experts – in similar vein to civil society and even members of the Parliament. Furthermore, the report argued that the legislator should be granted maximum freedom in choosing instruments beyond opposition and revocation, in fixing objection deadlines and the ability to be consulted by the Commission in preparing delegated acts. Also, the report expressed a desire to reach a common understanding with the other institutions on practical matters, such as standard recitals (European Parliament, 2010b).

Although negotiations on this common understanding were nearly complete in the summer of 2010, they were not concluded until December, as part of a package with the new rules on implementing acts (see further). In the meantime, however, the Parliament did manage to strike a deal with the Commission on access to expert meetings. In the Framework Agreement between these institutions, which is revised after each new Commission assumes office, it was agreed that members of the Parliament were also to be invited to preparatory expert meetings for delegated acts if representatives from all member states were also invited (European Parliament and European Commission, 2010).

Delegated acts: Reactions from the Council

The agreement on the pet animal regulation was a serious setback for the Council. Many member states had tried to secure a privileged position for member state experts, and they kept trying. Although referring to 'national' experts in the recitals of basic acts was unacceptable to the European Parliament, the Council insisted on at least referring to 'experts'. Also, the member states required an explicit statement to the effect that a common understanding on delegated acts did not replace, but instead added to the Commission's communication (which made explicit reference to national experts). Since the new rules on implementing acts dominated discussions in COREPER (see further), the regime for delegated acts was not a high-priority item.

The only incident relating to this file took place on 29 September 2010, when the Commission adopted its first delegated acts on energy labelling. The Commission had adopted its acts after first consulting member state experts and then civil society actors. The member states did not have a problem with the contents of these delegated acts. But the sequence of consultation caused Denmark, Germany and the United Kingdom to protest in COREPER by means of a non-paper, which was supported by many other member states. Since the member state experts were consulted first – not last – they felt that the member states had lost their privileged position: they would no longer be able to scrutinize the final Commission drafts. In the non-paper, the Commission was asked to consent to systematically consulting with national experts, presenting draft delegated acts as formal agenda items with clear deadlines for reaction, after consultation with civil society actors but before the final adoption of a measure. In COREPER, the Commission pledged to reflect on the sequence of consulting stakeholders. Although the Council did not use its political weapon of revocation in this case, this was a testimony to the vigilance of some member states with respect to accountability for delegated acts.

Delegated acts: The Common Understanding

The Common Understanding between the Parliament, Council and Commission on delegated acts went through the institutions together with the new regulation on implementing acts (see further). This mainly included the simultaneous, timely and appropriate transmission of relevant documents to the European Parliament and the Council, the carrying out of appropriate consultations at expert level, the choice between undetermined and determined delegation of powers which are tacitly renewable unless opposed by either of the institutions, a standard objection period of 2 + 2 months at least, no transmission of delegated acts during recess periods except in urgency, and standard recitals to be included in new basic acts to that effect. Also, the Commission made a statement pledging to prepare alignment of the acquis to delegated acts where appropriate, and to have this completed by 2014. The Common Understanding was formally adopted on 3 March 2011.

Negotiating the control of implementing acts

The negotiations on the implementing acts regime under Article 291 (TFEU) soon hardened spectacularly. Not only was there a multitude of contested issues, issues that had seemingly been settled at an early stage tended to flare anew later on.

Implementing acts: The Commission's first move

Following earlier calls that 'all three institutions should reach agreement on the Commission's forthcoming proposal' (Council, 2009a), the Commission presented its views to the other institutions in non-papers in November 2009 proposing revolutionary reforms.

First, given that Article 291 (TFEU) explicitly refers to member state control as opposed to Council control, and given that the two legislators are on an equal footing, the Commission abandoned the age-old principle of referral to the Council. Instead, resubmission of the same or an amended draft to the same committee was proposed.

Second, under the guise of simplification, the Commission wanted to reduce the number of voting procedures from three (advisory, management and regulatory) to two (advisory and a new examination procedure). But the proposed examination procedure came very close to the old management procedure, using similar voting rules but without Council referral. It provided for the automatic alignment of existing committee procedures to the new system, with all advisory procedures remaining intact and all regulatory and management procedures becoming examination procedures. This exercise of automatic alignment was proposed to avoid lengthy omnibus processes.

Third, the Commission argued that both legislators needed to be continuously informed and to receive all documents in order to control the Commission. This could be regarded as a variant to the Parliament's existing right of scrutiny. Fourth, the Commission wanted stricter criteria for choosing committee procedures in basic acts. In sum, the Commission sought to eliminate the Council as a forum, and to make it harder for the member states to impose consequences.

Implementing acts: Initial responses from the European Parliament and the Council

Until December 2009, discussions between the Council and the Commission focused on a transitional arrangement that would apply after the entry into force of the Lisbon Treaty (including Article 291 TFEU), because the regulation implementing Article 291 did not exist at the time (Council 2009b, c). The end result was a joint declaration by the three institutions to continue applying the old comitology decision except for the regulatory procedure with scrutiny. This effectively provided the Council with a status quo that would continue to be valid after the entry into force of the new Treaty (Council, 2009c). The Council could therefore afford to be patient.

The first time the Commission's intentions regarding Article 291 (TFEU) were discussed was on 15 January 2010, in a newly established Council 'Friends of the Presidency' group. Several, but not all, member states opposed the idea of automatic alignment. Also, in the run-up to the publication of the final Commission proposal for a new regulation, the Council's legal service commented repeatedly that a new regulation would be superfluous, given that the legal context as regards the old comitology system (excluding the regulatory procedure with scrutiny) had not changed.

Actors within the Parliament stressed the need for a better and more complete flow of information between the Commission and Parliament, and for maintaining the Parliament's ability to control the legality of implementing acts (European Parliament, 2010a).

Implementing acts: The Commission's second move

On 9 March 2010, the Commission officially submitted its legislative proposal for a new regulation on implementing acts (European Commission, 2010c). It was even more radical than the earlier non-papers, in several important respects. First, the proposal explicitly referred to the common commercial policy as a domain of application of the new regulation. Hitherto, the procedures of the committees established before the 1987 comitology Decision never had to be aligned to the generic system laid down in the 1987 Decision, so that the Council was effectively able to pick and choose the committees it wanted to align. In the end, nearly all committees were aligned, but many committees in the common commercial policy never were (see also European Commission, 2011b). Article 291 (3) (TFEU), however, explicitly states that the rules governing the committees that concern the control of implementing acts must be laid down in regulations. The Commission interpreted this clause in the Treaty to mean that all possible voting regimes were in fact covered by the same, single regulation, on which the voting regimes of all implementing committees were to be based. Automatic alignment for the committees on the common commercial policy, however, was overseen in earlier drafts, given that those committees were at no time subject to any generic comitology regime under the 1987, 1999 or 2006 Decisions.

Second, the Commission operationalized its preference for more clarity and rigour in choosing voting procedures in basic acts very strictly. It proposed to make the advisory procedure the general rule, and only to allow the use of the examination procedure in the domains of health, environment, and the common agricultural, fisheries and commercial policies, or in relation to implementing measures of general scope in other policy domains. Third, the Commission proposed to move provisions on using a written voting procedure (see Chapter 2) from the rules of procedure of the individual committees to the regulation itself.

Fourth, the Commission wanted to be able to immediately adopt urgent measures and get a committee opinion later. But in certain cases, the Commission proposed to retain the right to keep those measures in force even after a negative committee opinion, after which it would reconsult the committee. Finally, the proposal mentioned access to information by the Council and Parliament, but not a right of scrutiny. The information sent to the other institutions was to be the same as in the old comitology system, but the Commission also proposed that only the references to those documents, not the full information, should be made available to the general public (European Commission, 2010a).

In sum, the proposal sought to radically reduce accountability in all possible respects: less information, fewer discussions in committee and fewer consequences. The Council and Parliament were to be marginalized as forums, and the committees themselves – both in their capacity of actors as well as forums – would be weakened.

Implementing acts: Negotiations in the Council

The Commission's proposal was extensively discussed in a series of eight meetings in the Council's Friends of the Presidency group in March and April 2010 (Council, 2010). In particular, the member states objected to the weak position of the member states under the proposed examination procedure, as well as to the binding nature of the criteria for choosing voting procedures, to the lack of a control mechanism at the political level (i.e. the Council) for sensitive measures adopted after 'no opinion' in the examination procedure, to the lack of involvement of the Council, and to the proposed automatic alignment. In addition, several member states preferred to exclude the common commercial policy from the regulation and to continue to decide committee procedures in each basic act.

In response, the Commission indicated that it would be possible to keep the special regimes for commercial policy, as long as they were included in the new regulation. Also, it argued that it was impossible to maintain a role for the Council as an institution, since the formal competences lay with the member states by virtue of the wording in the Treaty. However, off the record, the Commission launched the idea of establishing a 'super committee' of high-level member state representatives to which salient issues could be referred. The workings of this committee, later to be dubbed the 'appeal committee', together with the issue of trade politics, were to stay on the Council and European Parliament's agendas for the remainder of the negotiations.

In the subsequent Friends of the Presidency meetings, all member states sought to keep intact at least some of the special procedures in the common commercial policy, and the idea of a super committee gained broad support. This new appeal body would convene if the Commission proved unable to adopt an implementing measure, but unwilling to submit an amended version to the same committee. In such cases, the appeal committee would decide on the original proposal by qualified majority. After a positive opinion, the Commission would have to adopt the measure; following a negative opinion, it would not be able to do so. After no opinion in the appeal committee, the Commission would be free to adopt or not to adopt its original draft measure, although one of the introductory recitals to the draft regulation states that the Commission may not go against a predominant position of the member states (i.e. a simple majority) in the appeal committee in particular policy fields.

Furthermore, nearly all member states found that automatic alignment would be acceptable only with stronger member state control under the examination procedure. This was arranged by adding a generic rule that a simple majority of member states would be able to block adoption of a Commission proposal. Also, extra clauses were added that in sum resembled the old regulatory procedure, but that were scattered through the articles on the examination procedure. These 'regulatory' clauses could optionally be triggered in specific instances where the basic act so provided. This, too, included a role for the appeal committee after a blocking minority.

Interestingly, a generic referral to the appeal committee after a negative vote by a simple majority of committee members was also included in this process. Hitherto, agreements to that effect were made in the form of a unilateral Commission statement, following the 1999 comitology decision stating that the Commission would seek a solution in cases where a 'predominant position' emerged in the committees. No conclusion on the matter could be reached in the Friends of the Presidency group, and by the end of May 2010 the dossier was forwarded to COREPER II (Council, 2010), after which the Belgian Presidency from 1 July moved the file to COREPER I.

From June onwards, however, two outstanding issues forwarded to COREPER and its preparatory Mertens Group turned out to be particularly tricky. First, the Spanish Presidency proposed that the appeal committee be chaired by a member state as opposed to the Commission. The member states were divided on the issue, with a number of strong member states supporting the proposal and others expressing no strong preferences on this matter. Confronted with the Commission's rigid attitude on the one hand, and Parliament's opposition to the proposal on the other, a majority of member states agreed on Commission chairmanship.

The second issue was the common commercial policy. Carving out external trade was unacceptable to the Commission, whereas keeping it in the regulation led to a stalemate in the Council. The discussion focused on the issues of anti-dumping and anti-subsidy measures on imports. Free-trade oriented Northern member states strongly favoured a committee procedure in which a simple majority could block the Commission, whereas the more protectionist Southern countries favoured the standard examination procedure (i.e. blockade by means of a qualified majority against). Since both camps had a blocking minority in the Council and since both were determined to find a permanent solution, this issue paralysed the negotiations. Solutions were explored in all sorts of variants, but it was not until September that the issue became somewhat less complicated, following a letter from Trade Commissioner De Gucht, which stated that exceptions to the standard voting rules were simply not acceptable to the Commission. Although this letter relegated a carve-out solution and special free-trade oriented voting schemes to the realm of 'the impossible', it did clarify the situation by declaring the blocking minority championed by the free-trade countries the only relevant obstacle to a final solution. This blocking minority was broken by crafting a special arrangement for multilateral safeguard measures within the new regulation – the crucial issue for Germany to accept the remainder of the text. Combined with the inclusion of a blocking simple minority in the appeal committee for the first 18 months regarding countervailing or anti-dumping measures, this package secured a qualified majority in the Council.

Furthermore, a variation on the original automatic alignment proposal was agreed upon at the very last minute. Alignments to the new delegated act regime must be examined on a case-to-case basis. The remaining advisory and management procedures were aligned to advisory and examination procedures, respectively, in the new system, whereas the regulatory procedures were to be aligned to examination procedures in which no opinion by the committee blocked the Commission as well. In sum, the old procedures remained intact for existing committees, only with the appeal committee assuming the role previously played by the Council. No generic rules were established about the level of participation in the meetings of the appeal committee, even though its first meeting on 29 March 2011 was attended by the member states' deputy permanent representatives.

The European Parliament's desire for a right of scrutiny, which was included in the original Commission non-papers but omitted from the official regulation initiative, appeared on the Council's agenda in September. For the most part, the member states saw no problem in granting this right to the European Parliament and Council.

Discussions in the Council thus centred on the ease by which the member states could impose consequences on the Commission, as well as on the identification of forums (i.e. the creation of a special appeal body). Moreover, the Council was quite successful in securing stronger voting rules than those envisaged by the Commission. The elements of information and discussion were not on the agenda.

Implementing acts: Negotiations in the European Parliament

Formal discussions in the European Parliament started in the Legal Affairs committee after the Commission officially presented its proposal on 9 March 2010. However, the discussions that took place on delegated acts in the same committee, allowed various initial reactions to be observed before this date. In the European Parliament's report on delegated acts, a resolution stated that 'parliament should retain a right of information concerning implementing acts, in as much as this would enable it to control their legality' (European Parliament, 2010b). This does not go beyond the right of information already proposed by the Commission in its formal proposal.

While discussions in the Legal Affairs committee got under way, all other Parliamentary committees were invited to give their opinion to the Legal Affairs committee. No less than 12 of these committees proposed amendments. Five (Agriculture, Fisheries, Transport and Tourism, Environment and Development) protested against automatic alignment, since they feared that comitology issues that previously did not fall under co-decision could now automatically fall under the implementing act scheme, without offering the legislator the opportunity to opt for a delegated act. The same five committees, but joined by the committees on the Internal Market and Consumer Affairs, International Trade, Economic Affairs and Constitutional Affairs, expressed a desire to maintain the *droit de regard* that the Parliament enjoyed under the old comitology system, either in unaltered or expanded form. The committees on Environment, Regional Development, Economic Affairs, Transport and Tourism, Internal Market, Foreign Affairs and Development requested a more extensive and more reliable flow of information from the Commission. Furthermore, several individual committees voiced a number of particular desires. The Environment committee proposed applying the examination procedure as the default procedure for all environment-related issues, and the Civil Liberties committee did likewise for their policy realm. The committee on International Trade, together with Development, Transport and Tourism, and Economic Affairs, requested access to committee meetings. The Foreign Affairs committee, while rejecting the idea of a *droit de regard*, wanted to be involved in the decision-making related to implementing acts on foreign aid. The Development committee, finally, expressed grievances about not having been able thus far to start using delegated acts for all measures relating to development. Comments from the European Parliament committees addressed all elements of accountability, generally preferring more information, discussion and abilities of imposing consequences for the European Parliament.

Szájer's draft report of 20 May 2010 referred to the following as 'main issues'. First, automatic alignment could only have a temporal effect – if agreed to at all – so that in each case, the choice between a delegated and an implementing act could be made anew. In this process, priority was to be given to files not falling under co-decision prior to the Lisbon Treaty. Second, information provision by the Commission was seen as crucial, including an obligation for the Commission to respond to statements made by the European Parliament and Council. Finally, the report questioned whether the criteria for choosing comitology procedures should be binding. The draft report also proposed a *droit de regard* for both the Council and European Parliament, but in the final report, this was not included as a main issue (European Parliament, 2010d). The draft report appeared to leave the issue of accountability consequences to the Council, focusing instead on information and discussion.

In the meantime, the Council started negotiations between the member states, and several actors within the European Parliament had informal contacts with the Commission and the Council Presidency. Throughout March and April of that year, the European Parliament communicated to the Commission and Council that it only had two red lines: no automatic alignment, and no role for the Council as an appeal body. On 5 July, while discussions in the Council focused on the appeal committee, the European Parliament added the chairmanship of the appeal committee by the Commission and absence of additional constraints on the Commission in the appeal committee as main points.

In September 2010, the *droit de regard* was put on the table for the first time, together with a proposal to evaluate the workings of the implementing act regime. In addition, Parliament objected to the article stating that the examination procedure should be the default procedure for foreign aid (European Parliament, 2010c). Although the proposed regulation did not preclude any choice between delegated and implementing acts in basic acts, the Development committee in the European Parliament saw this proposal as a political statement favouring implementing acts.

From that time onwards, the negotiations worked towards finding solutions. In a trialogue held on 22 October 2010, the Parliament agreed to the formula on the common commercial policy that had dominated discussions in COREPER for several months. In addition, Parliament was willing to accept an appeal committee chaired by the Commission, provided it was granted a *droit de regard* and that the alignment issue was resolved within the scope of the new regulation. Finally, the Commission accommodated the European Parliament on the issue of Development by means of a non-paper, stating that the Commission will 'associate the European Parliament up-stream' in the making of broad strategic objectives and outcomes. On 1 December, the JURI committee accepted the full package that had finally been negotiated by the Council, including removal of the time limits on the *droit de regard* and extending it to the Council, under the condition that the explicit referral to development aid issues in combination with implementing measures be deleted from the regulation (European Parliament, 2010e).

On 16 December 2010, the European Parliament formally adopted the compromise package at its first reading by an overwhelming majority of 567 votes to four (18 abstentions). In the Council, the compromise was formally enacted as a first reading decision on 14 February 2011, with the Netherlands and the United Kingdom abstaining, after which the Regulation was numbered 182/2011 and published two days later in the Official Journal.

Table 4.3 and Figure 4.3 summarize the committee powers as well as the accountability relationships set out in the post-Lisbon comitology

Table 4.3 Committee powers in the post-Lisbon comitology system

Procedure	Committee stage	Appeal stage
Delegated acts	No binding consequences	European Parliament or Council normally have 2 + 2 months to veto individual acts
Implementing acts:		European Parliament or Council can revoke delegation
Advisory	No binding consequences	No appeal
Examination (normal variant)	If simple or qualified majority against: referral to appeal committee	Appeal committee blocks adoption by qualified majority against
Examination (regulatory variant)	If no qualified majority in favour: referral to appeal committee	As above, except for multilateral safeguard measures in external trade: blocks in absence of a qualified majority in favour
Examination (anti-dumping variant)	If qualified majority against: referral to appeal committee If simple majority but no qualified majority against: referral to appeal committee after member state consultations	Appeal committee blocks adoption by qualified majority against

Source: European Parliament and Council Regulation 2011/182/EU; Common Understanding of 3 March 2011.

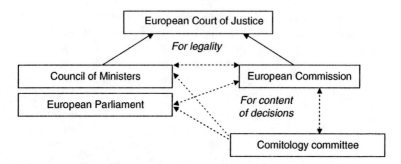

Figure 4.3 Accountability in the post-Lisbon comitology system

system. Compared to the pre-Lisbon system, there are many similarities, but also many exceptions, to the general rules. What could have been a perfect opportunity for both further simplifying the comitology system as well as strengthening accountability in the end led to a Byzantine arrangement. Moreover, the delegated acts system has put stronger legislative accountability mechanisms in place that tend to be incidental by their very nature, whereas the more hands-on accountability through committees has been weakened.

Conclusion: An increasingly complex accountability system

In sum, 50 years of negotiations on the set-up of comitology have shown that accountability is somewhat of a thorny issue. Institutional interests differ significantly. The Commission, as an actor, prefers minimal control, while especially the Council prefers maximal scrutiny powers. Throughout history, the Council has always managed to make sure that the comitology regime includes stronger mechanisms for imposing consequences than preferred by the Commission. Still, the Commission has very slowly managed to get rid of the strongest voting procedures. The European Parliament, in turn, prefers equality over accountability as such: it either prefers to have the same powers as the member states in the Council, or it prefers a minimal role for member state committees in holding the Commission to account.

Against this historical backdrop, the case study of the post-Lisbon comitology reform provides some remarkable new insights. Most notably, the Council seems to focus exclusively on consequences, while the European Parliament addresses all elements of accountability. What is more, the

European Parliament has broken with a nearly 50-year-old tradition: namely that of bargaining for more rights to impose consequences across the board of comitology. With implementing acts, it could well have bargained for stronger scrutiny powers, yet it did not, even though the European Parliament had now become a full co-decision maker in the set-up of the system (Christiansen and Dobbels, 2012) and many parliamentary committees would, in fact, have preferred such powers. The only logical explanation is that in the end, it attributes more importance to its new powers of overseeing delegated acts, and believes it can successfully bargain for including delegated acts in new legislation, as opposed to implementing acts.

The resulting accountability system, in the end, is a messy one. The Treaty mentions criteria for including either delegated or implementing procedures in basic acts, but in practice, there is a grey zone between the two, as the discussion on foreign aid has shown. The delegated act system took away the committees' powers to impose consequences, and granted these powers to the legislative institutions. While no committees have been formally established, they exist in practice, and informal agreements have been made on the sequencing of advice, on exchanging information and on participation rights – information that is crucial for the legislators for exercising control. The informality of this regime makes it easy for the Commission to bend the informal rules and avoid accountability.

The new regulation on implementing acts is very unclear as to the consequences that the implementing committees are able to impose. Straightforward criteria for blocking Commission proposals in the old comitology system have been replaced by a list of partially overlapping criteria in the new system. On a more practical note, the regulation first presents standard voting rules, which are subsequently found to be accompanied by complicated exceptions, and even exceptions to exceptions.

The picture of accountability relations depicted in Figure 4.2 largely remained the same after the 2011 reform. However, the dashed lines, representing incomplete accountability relationships, have become increasingly complex. The delegated acts system may provide for less systematic scrutiny than before, because the status of its expert groups is unclear. Parliament's *droit de regard* can now also be applied by the Council, also for non-co-decision files. Parliament still cannot oversee the content of individual implementing measures whereas the member states in the committee can. The Council no longer serves as an appeal body following a negative committee opinion: this task has now been assumed by an 'appeal committee' of high-ranking member state officials and chaired by the Commission.

All forums in the system have powers to impose consequences, but they are not completely free to decide when to do so. Moving on from system-level accountability towards accountability at the level of the committees, this begs the question as to the degree to which the European Parliament and the committees can and actually do exercise their role as accountability forums in practice. Do the committees effectively constrain the behaviour of the Commission, and in what ways does the European Parliament make use of the information stemming from the committees in order to hold the Commission accountable? These two questions are the focus of the next chapter.

5
Committee-Level Accountability: System Meets Practice

Introduction

The design of the comitology system is far from parsimonious. It is not just 'institutionally schizophrenic' (Brandsma, Curtin and Meijer, 2008) in the sense that it is a device pushed mainly by the Council in order to 'rein in' the supranational executive competences of the Commission. From its very inception, the comitology system has been Janus-faced in its accountability tasks. On the one hand, the committees are designed to be the control devices of the member states over the Commission. From the moment the very first committee was established, the Council has systematically created stricter procedures than the Commission had proposed. This has led, for instance, to the creation of regulatory procedures in the 1960s, and to the introduction of member state expert groups for delegated acts in the 2011 reform.

But on the other hand, the committees have, in practice, become jointly responsible with the Commission for the executive measures that are eventually adopted. Because of the voting rules that have formal consequences for adopting implementing acts, as well as the extensive and permanent dialogue between the Commission and member state experts for all types of measures, the comitology committees are not just controllers but rather co-creators of policy outputs. This is one of the reasons why the European Parliament has constantly pushed, with increasing success in recent years, to become an accountability forum in relation to comitology decision-making.

This chapter empirically addresses these two accountability relationships. It takes the formal design of the accountability system as a starting point and investigates its actual functioning at the *committee level*. Do the committees effectively constrain the behaviour of the Commission, and how does the European Parliament make use of the information stemming from the committees in order to hold the Commission to account?

These two questions are investigated on the basis of different types of data. The first section of this chapter analyses the relation between the committees and the Commission on the basis of survey data collected among committee participants. It taps different types of interaction between the Commission and the committee participants, showing that the committees indeed have a moderating effect on the Commission; to some extent perhaps an even more moderating effect than would be expected on the basis of the voting rules alone.

The second section focuses on the relation between the committees and the European Parliament, and follows the paper trail from the committees to the MEPs. It shows how various actors within the European Parliament deal with this and filter out information along the way. In the end, however, the European Parliament rarely uses the formal and informal political rights with respect to comitology affairs it fought so hard to obtain. On a day-to-day basis, its interest in comitology is tepid at the most.

Comitology and the Commission: Mutual dependence in action

Observers of comitology have noted that there is a range of different types of behaviour within the committees that can be interpreted as informal norms of decision-making. These informal workings, characterizing the everyday workings of comitology, affect the degree to which the committees hold the Commission to account in actual practice. To be sure, these informal workings are complementary to some parameters that are fixed as a matter of system choice. Examples of such fixed parameters include the fact that the committees are chaired by the Commission, that the Commission provides for the committees' secretariat, that certain voting rules apply, that draft measures are formally presented by the Commission, and that in its capacity as chair of the committee meetings, the Commission can play around with the timing for putting a draft measure forward for a vote (see Chapter 2). But on a behavioural level, there is substantial variation in the interaction patterns between committee members and the Commission, as well as among the committee members themselves. This affects the modes by which – and the degree to which – the committees in practice hold the Commission to account.

Intergovernmental negotiation and deliberative supranationalism

A rich body of literature has accrued around the practices within comitology committees. Some authors focus on role orientations of committee members as a proxy for their behaviour in Brussels (Egeberg, Schäfer and Trondal, 2003; Trondal, 2002; see also Chapter 6). Others have tapped interaction patterns more broadly through interviews (Joerges and Neyer, 1997b; Alfé, Christiansen and Piedrafita, 2008), through large-scale surveys (Sannerstedt, 2005; Blom-Hansen and Brandsma, 2009) or by observing committee meetings directly (Geuijen et al., 2008).

What these studies have in common is that they tend to portray comitology decision-making along the lines of two images that have dominated the literature since the early 1990s: intergovernmental negotiation and deliberative supranationalism. The first image maintains that the committees provide every opportunity for member state control of the Commission through the use of formal rules. This control can be exercised either directly by the Council, such as is the case in the delegated acts regime, or by the implementing acts committees. The voting procedures of both the Council and the committees have a binding effect on the Commission, allowing member state representatives to exert influence on the Commission throughout the executive phase of policymaking as well. The Commission can only go ahead and implement its proposed policies in the case of a sufficiently positive vote, or, with regard to delegated acts, if no opposition is expected. The latter may be signalled by the member state experts with whom the Commission is required to consult before adopting delegated acts. In other words, the negotiations between the member state representatives under the shadow of the voting procedure used are crucial to creating acceptable solutions.

The intergovernmental negotiation perspective largely derives from the school of rational choice institutionalism, and emphasizes the strategic use that actors make of the formal arrangements. Studies of the daily operation of selected comitology committees indeed find such strategic use. A relatively well-known instance of this occurs when the Commission uses its advantageous position under some voting procedures in order to push GMO regulation through the comitology system (Hofmann and Toeller, 1997; Bradley, 1998). Other studies have focused more on the degree to which national preferences dominate committee discussions. In several cases, they found that, in fact, they actually do (Daemen and Van Schendelen, 1998; Philip, 1998). The finding that national identities precede European identities with respect to role orientations of committee participants (Egeberg, Schäfer and Trondal, 2003, 32; Trondal, 2004, 23–4) also neatly fits into this line of research.

The deliberative supranationalist perspective stands in sharp contrast to this view of comitology decision-making. Given the technical nature of the issues discussed in committee meetings, the member states normally send their policy experts in the relevant area to the committee meetings. According to this perspective, therefore, it is not the formal rules underlying the system that control decision-making, but rather the power of arguments on the basis of expertise. Comitology is an opportunity for member state actors and representatives from European institutions to interact and formalize solutions that produce the best technical results for all. In fact, the mutual learning effects stemming from interaction between Commission and member state administrators have already been noted and even applauded by the European Parliament in the early 1960s (Bergström, 2005, p. 54–7). In this case, it is deliberation that is the balancing mechanism between Commission and member states in comitology.

The strength of the deliberative supranationalist perspective in studies on comitology may stem from the fact that it is not only an empirical perspective that is truly different from the rational choice institutionalist perspective on the functioning of control mechanisms, but also that it is a normative one in its own right. Its chief promoters, Joerges and Neyer (1997a, b), argue that deliberative supranationalism is a superior form of policymaking given that national administrators, bounded by the limits of their own jurisdictions, have very few mechanisms of their own to account for pan-European effects of their decisions that affect the workings of the common market. Comitology, so they argue, provides an excellent platform for exchanging views on one particular subject and for working towards consensus on the basis of expertise. In this regard they have substantiated, on the basis of evidence gathered from one particular committee, that comitology indeed works like this in practice. Others, too, have found that the committees are used as areas for deliberation in the sense that arguing rather than bargaining characterizes the committees' deliberations (Geuijen et al., 2008).

Several studies present intergovernmental negotiation and supranational deliberation as two poles on the same dimension (Egeberg, Schäfer and Trondal, 2003; Pollack, 2003a). Although analytically different, indeed, research into the full spectrum of committees shows that this, in fact, is a false dichotomy. In some committees, indeed, either deliberation or negotiation dominates, but there are many cases where both types of interaction occur regularly. Equally well, there are tame committees in which neither seems to occur to a great degree (Blom-Hansen and Brandsma, 2009, 730). The two perspectives, thus, are not mutually exclusive, which means that in practice both forms of interaction take place, creating different behavioural logics upon which the committee participants base their assessments of the Commission's proposals – and then pass judgement.

The Commission's role in comitology

It is noteworthy that all of the aforementioned research taps into the actual behaviour of member state representatives, also including their perceptions on the behaviour of other member state representatives, but that information on the behaviour of the Commission is lacking for the most part. But from the perspective of accountability this is the most salient aspect: how accommodating towards member state representatives is the Commission really? The Commission, for its part, repeatedly points out that the committees and the Commission work together in perfect harmony: very few delegated acts so far have been opposed by the Parliament or Council, and only very few issues have been referred to the Council or to the appeal committee due to a negative vote result. Figures on a yearly basis range from three to 17, which is only a very small portion of the total of 2,000 to 2,500 measures per year passing through comitology (European Commission, 2002 to 2008, 2009a, 2010b, 2011a). But the number of referrals to the Council is probably not the best indicator: it only shows that the committees rarely impose consequences. During committee proceedings, the Commission can work towards the barest possible majority, or take into account the opinions of states that are irrelevant to the outcome of the vote. Nothing is known about the number of items withdrawn before a vote, or about amendments made to draft acts, or about the degree of control by the member states of the Commission through comitology, and how far the Commission is willing to accommodate them.

In order to be able to show a complete picture of the workings of deliberation, negotiation and accommodation by the Commission, a survey was carried out among the Dutch and Danish spokespersons in all comitology committees that were active in the year 2005.[1] Although the system was reformed in the year 2011, this study still yields substantial insight into the daily functioning of the system, given that the voting procedures have not changed materially in the domain of implementing acts, and that all existing committees were included in the domain of the survey. In Denmark, 191 respondents received a questionnaire and 161 responded. For the Netherlands, these figures were 167 and 133, respectively. The overall response rate was 82 per cent. The missing 18 per cent created no non-response bias (for further details on the survey, see Blom-Hansen, 2007 and Brandsma, 2007).

Deliberation, negotiation and accommodation

The aim of the analysis presented here is not to establish causal links, but rather to provide an indication of how the daily practices of committee control over the Commission are to be characterized. What is the degree to which negotiation, deliberation and accommodation occur, and to what degree do they coincide?

Table 5.1 shows descriptive statistics for each of the indicators associated, respectively, with intergovernmental bargaining, deliberative supranationalism and the accommodating attitude of the Commission in the committees. Besides this, the table also shows the same statistics for the scales associated with the concepts as a whole. In order to increase comparability, the aggregated scales are the same as those used for different purposes in earlier studies (Blom-Hansen and Brandsma, 2009; Brandsma and Blom-Hansen, 2010; Blom-Hansen, 2011b).

A number of interesting observations can be made from the figures presented here. Beginning with the first block of indicators, the dominance of national interests in the committee meetings stands out, but this does not generally coincide with hard bargaining. Although there are certainly several committees where intergovernmental bargaining is the dominant mode of interaction (Blom-Hansen and Brandsma, 2009, 730), on the whole, bargaining takes place at only a moderate degree. This is reflected by a score of 2.65 on a five-point scale. On the other hand, deliberation occurs to a somewhat stronger degree. Here, all the indicators are in the same range, and the aggregate position is 3.98 on a five-point scale. The Commission's attitude appears to be moderately mediating. With a score that is half a point above the mid-point of the scale, the Commission does not completely disregard member state preferences. Rather, it makes some effort to get the entire forum on board, although it by no means goes all the way.

The high scores on, especially, deliberation and to some degree also the moderately accommodating role played by the Commission are all indicative of a low level of confrontation between member state representatives and the Commission within the comitology committees. To a large degree, the committees work towards joint solutions, and participants can be convinced to change their position on the basis of good arguments. Obviously, all this takes place in the form of proposals presented and explained by the Commission, since this is part of

Table 5.1 Interaction modes within comitology committees

	Mean	Standard Deviation
Intergovernmental bargaining		
In the meetings of my comitology committee		
... compromises are normally political horse trades	2.43	0.977
... it is really the large countries that decide	2.63	1.057
... the participants often resort to bluffing	1.83	0.840
... national interests dominate our work	3.71	0.883
4-item scale of intergovernmental bargaining (Chronbach's alpha: 0.61)*	2.65	0.647
Deliberative supranationalism		
In the meetings of my comitology committee		
... participants can freely express their opinion	4.61	0.713
... it happens that participants are persuaded by good arguments to change their position	3.50	1.012
... arguments on common solutions are especially important	3.87	0.926
... the participants normally present detailed arguments for their positions	3.91	0.853
4-item scale of deliberative supranationalism (Chronbach's Alpha: 0.50)*	3.98	0.560
Accommodating attitudes (Commission)		
In the meetings of my comitology committee, the Commission is		
... the one who mediates	3.55	0.896
... the one who makes sure that everybody feels comfortable	3.36	0.954
... the one who makes sure that the result is satisfactory to everyone	3.57	0.748
3-item scale of the Commission's attitude (Chronbach's Alpha: 0.71)*	3.49	0.690

* For additive index of items mentioned earlier.
Note: All items are Likert scale statements to which the respondents could answer 'disagree', 'partly disagree', 'neither agree nor disagree', 'partly agree', and 'agree'. Aggregate indices were rescaled to a five-point scale.

the constitutional fabric of the comitology system. Although national interests are clearly present during meetings, this does not translate into hard bargaining sessions. In this regard, the data supports the image of the Commission and the committees as joint decision-makers, as opposed to a 'mini-Council' or a system in which the Commission does not accept solutions deviating from its own original proposal.

This interpretation is further bolstered when we look at the degree to which the three forms of control coincide. Table 5.2 presents the correlations between all three scales. It is important to note here that the correlations do not imply causality, since all phenomena can and in fact do occur at the same time. That is, committees may well behave in a deliberative fashion because the Commission adopts an accommodating attitude, but it is also just as possible for the chain of events to run the other way, or even in opposite directions between committees. For the purposes of this analysis, that is, to characterize the mode by which the committees balance the Commission's powers in practice, causality is not a primary concern.

Table 5.2 shows that all modes of behaviour correlate in one way or another. The moderately strong, but highly significant, link between the Commission's attitude and deliberative interactions within the committees suggests that the Commission is less accommodating when the committees are less deliberative and/or vice versa. Apparently, deliberation and accommodation to a large extent occur together.

The picture is different with respect to intergovernmental bargaining. While the Commission might have been expected to make attempts to mediate between the member states in pursuit of solutions, posing, as it were, as an 'honest broker', in comitology quite the opposite is true. The more member state representatives bargain among each other in order to secure the best possible deal, the less accommodating the Commission behaves, allowing the member state representatives to sort out their differences among themselves. Of course the link may also be inverted: when the Commission fails to regard the concerns of the individual member states, they will fall back on bargaining among each other.

Obviously, the existence of positive or negative correlations, especially when they are weak or moderately strong as in all the cases presented here, does not mean in a deterministic sense that the said phenomena are all sides of the same coin. Given that the correlations are not very high, there must be many committees where these phenomena do not

Table 5.2 Correlations between modes of interaction within comitology

	Deliberative supranationalism	Commission as accommodator
Intergovernmental bargaining	–0.114*	–0.149**
Deliberative supranationalism	–	0.346***

Note: * sign. < 0.10, ** sign. < 0.05, *** sign. < 0.01.

go together. The figures are thus only representative of the general pattern among the full population of committees.

Having said that, it may be concluded that in general, the Commission and the committees work actively and well together, and that comitology is not just a case of peaceful coexistence. Of course, there are cases where the member states clearly dominate, but the dominant picture of the practices within comitology is certainly not one of intense conflict. The relatively high scores on deliberation and accommodation across the full range of committees are indicative of constructive mutual dependence at work. All of this naturally takes place under the shadow of a future vote or of legislative scrutiny, but existing evidence so far shows that the *strength* of a voting procedure does not correlate with the degree of accommodation demonstrated by the Commission during the committees' deliberations (Brandsma and Blom-Hansen, 2010, 505–9).

In terms of accountability, comitology indeed caters to mutual dependence between the member states and the Commission, but this goes beyond the control that is embedded in the voting procedures. Apparently, the pay-off for the Commission is larger when its proposals can count on more than a bare minimum of support, and the Commission does go some way to accommodate all member states. In this regard, the committees balance the Commission's powers; one might even go so far as to refer to cooperation. But does the European Parliament lose out on this close intertwining of European and national executive actors?

The European Parliament and comitology: From institutional interests to daily practices

The committees' internal working norms presented previously further underscore that the committees do more than merely control the Commission's exercise of its powers; they effectively participate in its executive decision-making. With 35 to 50 per cent of all Union decisions, directives and regulations made through comitology committees, comitology is a considerable decision-maker in its own right. Ever since the early 1960s, the European Parliament has taken an activist stance against it and has used all formal and informal opportunities that it had to gain greater scrutiny powers over comitology, including freezing budgets and holding up legislation (see Chapter 4).

From a checks and balances perspective on accountability, the European Parliament may be regarded as a forum able to balance the power emanating from the comitology system, given that it has a constitutional role to control the Commission. More practically, it is the only institutional forum at the European level that is possibly able to control comitology decision-making (Curtin and Egeberg, 2008, 652). At the same time, the popular control perspective of accountability has also steadily gained relevance in this regard since 1992, when the European Parliament acquired the power to co-decide on European legislation, while decisions on its implementation continued to be routed via committees of member state representatives.

The European Parliament's quest for more scrutiny powers can be said to have been quite successful given its victories in parts of the comitology system (see Chapter 4). Now that it has formally obtained a role as an accountability forum, the more practical question now becomes that of how it plays this role in practice. This section empirically examines this matter. After a more detailed account of the European Parliament's information and sanctioning rights, the analysis follows the paper trail from comitology committees to the MEPs. On the basis of interview data it shows how various actors within the European Parliament deal with this and filter out information along the way.

The European Parliament's information rights

For the European Parliament, the availability of sufficient and useful information is an essential asset, as it is for any parliament. To fulfil its legislative function, it requires expert information for making effective decisions. For its role as an accountability forum, which is of prime concern here, it needs information about the wheeling and dealing of the executive. From a checks and balances perspective on accountability, for instance, it needs information that reveals whether or not the executive has exceeded its discretionary powers that were specified in legislation. From a popular control perspective, by contrast, information about the input and output of executive decision-making processes would be needed, in order for the legislator to be able to judge what particular preferences have in fact been translated into policies and how, and what have not (Bovens, 't Hart and Schillemans, 2008, 230–3).

Although the European Parliament obtained commitments from the Commission on the forwarding of comitology documents in the 1990s, it was not until the adoption of the1999 Comitology Decision that these were truly formalized and coupled to specific political rights. However, the number of documents that had and still have to be forwarded was extraordinarily large. These include at least three documents per committee meeting (an agenda, a summary record and an attendance list), plus at least an additional two per implementing measure (the measure itself and the vote result). This amounts to about 8,000 documents per year, not counting different language versions. Parliament's victory in obtaining some measure of recognition as an accountability forum in 1999 therefore also necessitated a few practical arrangements on document forwarding. While the 1999 Comitology Decision did specify which particular types of documents the European Parliament was entitled to receive, it did not mention conditions and procedures under which those documents were to be forwarded.

In October 2000, Parliament and the Commission concluded a bilateral inter-institutional agreement to this effect (European Parliament and European Commission, 2000). This agreement upheld the 1999 Decision in specifying the types of documents that Parliament is to receive: draft agendas for meetings, the results of voting, a list of authorities to which the member state representatives belong, summary records of the committees' discussions and draft implementing measures that were submitted to the committees, the latter only when based on a co-decision act. The agreement further stated that Parliament was to receive those documents at the same time and on the same conditions as the member state representatives in the committees. The agreement did not, however, provide for making available the elaborate versions of the committees' minutes. Nevertheless, the Court of Justice ruled a few years earlier that Parliament could request access to those elaborate minutes, as well as to draft implementing measures that were not based upon a co-decision act.[2] At the time, because the European Parliament had no right of scrutiny over non co-decision based implementing measures, those documents could be requested for information purposes only. The Commission also agreed to forward such documents via email.

Extra information agreements were made between the European Parliament and the Commission in 2001 and 2003 for measures relating to financial services. This relates to the European Parliament's special powers of scrutiny in that field. The Commission and Parliament agreed to set up regular meetings only for financial services between the two institutions: monthly meetings between the secretariat of the European Parliament's committee on Economic Affairs and the Commission services in DG Internal Market, and regular meetings between the Commissioner and the coordinators and rapporteurs within the Economic Affairs committee (European Commission, 2001). An extra agreement was made to the effect that Commission officials would inform the European Parliament of the discussions in comitology committees and that they would be obliged to answer any questions from the European Parliament on such discussions, either orally or in writing. All in all, these constituted informal but very specific accountability agreements on transmitting information and organizing discussions between the two institutions.

With the conclusion of the 2006 Comitology Decision, which allowed for stronger parliamentary scrutiny under the regulatory procedure with scrutiny, the European Parliament sought to ensure better access to comitology information. It successfully bargained for yet another interinstitutional agreement with the Commission, replacing the 2000 agreement (European Parliament and European Commission, 2008). The 2008 agreement in fact reaffirms the agreements made in the year 2000, and also semi-codifies the extra arrangements that were made in the financial services sector. The only new element is that full minutes are now explicitly classified as confidential documents, so that leaking these can be punished. Also, the 2008 agreement refers to the establishment by the Commission of a new document register containing all documents forwarded from the Commission to the European Parliament, specifying the stage of the procedure of decision-making and timetable information. This register is directly accessible to the European Parliament and its services. Nevertheless, the agreement also states that the European Parliament will continue to receive individual documents by email.

Interestingly, the delegated acts procedure, under which the European Parliament has most extensive scrutiny powers, also comes with very few and unspecific information rights. This is because the committee system for delegated acts is an informal system (see Chapter 4). Table 5.3 shows the European Parliament's information rights regarding comitology, including the restrictions in the application of these rights.

In sum, Parliament is meant to receive all the information that it needs, both from a popular control and from a checks and balances perspective, even though for delegated acts the agreements are less specific due to the delegated acts committees' informal character. The information can be used to see which interests were translated into the eventual outcomes, for what reasons, and how. This, however, needs to be linked to actual sanctioning mechanisms before this information is useful within an accountability relationship.

The European Parliament's sanction repertoire

The European Parliament has several means at its disposal by which it can oppose comitology measures. Two of these are very specific rights

Table 5.3 Overview of the European Parliament's information rights for comitology

Pre-Lisbon comitology and post-Lisbon implementing acts regime

2000 Agreement		2008 Agreement	
Rights	**Restrictions**	**Rights**	**Restrictions**
Agendas	None	Same as in 2000, but also: Minutes	Same as in 2000, but classified as confidential
Vote results	Only generic results; not as per member state		
Attendance lists	Only organizations, no names or contact details	Access to document database	Maintained by Commission
Summary records	None, but documents are less specific and complete than minutes	Information on committee discussions	From 2003 and for financial services only
Draft measures	Only if the act is based on a co-decision act. If not, on special request and for information only.	Q&A with COM staff about committee discussions	From 2003 and for financial services only
Minutes	On special request only; Commission decides.	Three-level discussions	From 2001 and for financial services only

Post-Lisbon delegated acts regime

Rights	Restrictions
Appropriate contacts at administrative level	None
Documents on expert consultations	Selection of documents not specified
Relevant documents	'Relevance' not defined
Final delegated acts	None; no transmissions during recess except urgency measures
Advance notification of urgency measures	Informal notification; insofar foreseeable

that are tailor-made for comitology, and two more are generic rights, which the European Parliament can always use at its own discretion.

1. The *droit de regard* or *Right of Scrutiny (RoS)*: This right can only be exercised when overseeing implementing acts, not delegated acts. It allows the European Parliament to express its opposition to implementing acts, but only when these exceed the implementing powers provided for in basic legislation. Opposition can only be expressed by means of a resolution that is not binding on the Commission, and before the entry into force of the Lisbon, non co-decision based executive acts were excluded from this right. Additionally, until the entry into force of the 2011 Comitology Regulation, the Parliament also had a right to direct such a non-binding resolution to the Council only for regulatory committees in the rare event of them not having approved a draft measure, thereby increasing the chances of a Council veto in the appeal stage of the committee procedure. Normally, all such resolutions are initiated and adopted by the relevant parliamentary committee, after which plenary votes by means of an absolute majority of its component members.[3] This instrument thus only allows for quasi-legal control and the conditions are very strict.

    The European Parliament made little use of this right in the first decade of its existence: only nine times (European Commission, 2002 to 2008, 2009a, 2010b). This has a number of reasons: the *droit de regard* does not apply to all comitology decision-making; there is only one possible reason for objection that is extremely restrictive; and because both majorities in the European Parliament committee and in plenary are required, both within one month, while the European Parliament only has plenary meetings once a month to begin with.

2. The *delegated act procedure* and the *Regulatory Procedure with Scrutiny (RPS)*: These procedures, too, allow the European Parliament to oppose a draft measure, but its opposition is of a binding character. More grounds than just the Commission exceeding its powers are at issue. The European Parliament has unlimited grounds for objections, and it can even revoke delegation to the Commission completely. These consequences are only available for overseeing delegated acts.

    The pre-Lisbon Regulatory Procedure with Scrutiny (RPS) can be seen as the predecessor of this procedure. However, the latter is to be phased out by the year 2014. Under the RPS, Parliament may only object because a draft measure exceeds the Commission's implementing powers, because it is not compatible with the aim or content of the original co-decision act, or because it does not respect the principles of subsidiarity or proportionality. The route resolutions under this regime that must be followed is identical to that of *droit de regard* resolutions, but the time limits are wider. The parliamentary committee usually has two months to initiate a resolution, which can be extended by another two months for adopting it in plenary. The '2 + 2 months' formula is a post-Lisbon innovation (see Chapter 4); the RPS regime included a three-month window for completing the entire process.[4]

The question of which of the aforementioned two rights applies depends on the type of delegation of powers that is laid down in the original co-decision act, and therefore is subject of legislative bargaining (see Pollack 2003a, 130–144; 2003b; Bergström, 2005, p. 209–49; Vos, 1997; Franchino, 2000b; Héritier and Moury, 2011). The first right applies to implementing acts, while the second right applies to delegated acts (and to RPS issues for as long as the corresponding acts in the acquis have not yet been aligned to the delegated act regime). For matters not under the co-decision regime, neither of the two special rights applied up to the 2011 reform. Yet beyond these two sanctioning instruments, the European Parliament has a wider repertoire available.

3. The right to *make statements*: The European Parliament does not always need to follow the previous procedures in order to adopt resolutions. It also has the right to adopt resolutions in a general sense so as to make political statements. No time limits apply to those. Even though they do not produce binding effects, they may still have an impact because of the strong political message resolutions give. Resolutions have to follow the same route as the aforementioned specific resolutions, from individual MEPs, via a committee, to plenary.[5] A telling example is the Commission decision to put body scanners on the list of allowed security measures in airports. The Transport committee of the European Parliament decided not to formally object to the measure, but the Civil Liberties committee drafted a resolution against the use of body scanners, which was accepted in plenary. The Commission took notice of this message and decided to withdraw body scanners from the list (Hardacre and Damen, 2009).

4. *Bargaining*: Parliamentary committees (primarily) deal with legislative proposals. Therefore, they have the opportunity to express their grievances with executive decision-making in legislative negotiations with the other institutions on related issues. Because many pieces of

legislation have to be revised after a number of years, the other institutions can expect stronger demands from Parliament if it feels unhappy about the adopted executive measures. Similarly, parliamentary committees can also threaten to draft a resolution and rally support under the delegated acts scheme unless the Commission makes certain other commitments. This is an informal process, tagged by some as a 'de facto right of amendment' (Kaeding and Hardacre, 2010, p. 15).

The key actors in all of these four options are the parliamentary committees. Resolutions have to be adopted in plenary, but they need to be initiated in the parliamentary committees. As the next paragraph will show in greater detail, they are in fact the gatekeepers in holding comitology decision-making to account.

The European Parliament's information practices

The previous section showed a clear increase in both the scrutiny powers of the European Parliament as well as in the amount of information it receives. The sheer number of comitology meetings per year (about 1,000), the number of measures discussed in them (about 2,000 to 2,500) and the short time the European Parliament usually has to adopt resolutions when it is able to do so (one to three or four months) already form an indication of the time pressure under which Parliament has to operate. This begs the question of how the European Parliament deals in practice with its role as an accountability forum. An answer was sought in the interviews held in the European Parliament in 2010. Six interviews were held with staff members of the European Parliament's committees working on most of comitology's policies, who can be regarded as the gatekeepers to MEPs where comitology affairs are concerned (Kaeding and Hardacre, 2010, 9). Two additional interviews were held with staff members working on more horizontal affairs within the European Parliament. These interviews shed light on the following questions:

- How is the flow of information organized within the European Parliament?
- Who, in practice, deals with incoming information on comitology, and how is this information treated on a day-to-day basis?
- And how are MEPs finally made aware of the wheeling and dealing of the comitology committees?

Information on comitology committee proceedings follows a lengthy route from the Commission DGs that manage the comitology committees, via several Commission and Parliamentary services, to the responsible parliamentary committees. The European Parliament organized a police-patrol form of oversight for itself, but in a decentralized form (see further in McCubbins and Schwartz, 1984; Ogul and Rockman, 1990). In addition, a part of this information is also released to the general public through an Internet repository. This repository is by no means complete (Brandsma, Curtin and Meijer, 2008), but it can be used by various organizations to draw attention to certain issues of interest. Figure 5.1 shows a diagram of the entire information regime as it operates in practice.

The European Parliament has gradually learnt to cope with the massive amount of incoming documents, which is reflected in the allocation of tasks and responsibilities of staff members. A key actor in this respect, albeit one without any policy responsibilities, is Parliament's Receptions and Referrals Office. This unit is effectively Parliament's mailbox: all documents sent to Parliament, whether by regular mail or electronically, are received here. From here they are forwarded to the relevant

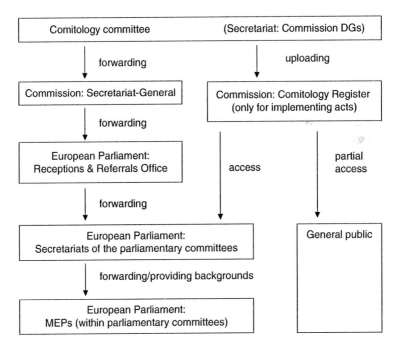

Figure 5.1 Information flow from comitology committee to MEP
Sources: European Parliament and European Commission (2008); European Parliament (2009b); Rules of Procedure of the European Parliament: Rule 88, Respondents 3, 5 and 8.

people in the European Parliament. For comitology documents, these are the staff in the secretariats of the parliamentary committees that were involved in drafting the original piece of legislation upon which the Commission's executive measures are based.

The system of how to forward the vast number of comitology documents has evolved gradually. Initially, the Commission sent its documents as email attachments without putting the topic of the message in the subject line. The Receptions and Referrals office simply forwarded all documents without systematically organizing them (Respondent 2). Impractical as this was, it took until 2006 before the need for a more systematic document handling system became pressing due to the introduction of the RPS procedure (Respondent 5). A new software package – 'EPGreffe' – introduced in May 2009 eased the workload of the Receptions and Referrals Office, as this enabled the Commission's secretariat-general to upload small packets of documents into it. The Receptions and Referrals Office then selects to whom these documents are to be forwarded, and also checks if, where necessary, all language versions are actually included in the document packets (Respondent 8). The appropriate parliamentary committee secretariat then receives the package of documents in an email attachment (Respondents 1, 2, 4 to 8).

Parallel to this, the Commission also started making the same information available in its own databases, which the European Parliament can log into and retrieve documents. This is the same database that the Commission uses for making available information to the general public, but with more extensive access to the parliamentary staff. The advantage of this register is that related or additional documents can be located more easily. Nevertheless, most European Parliament administrators use the information that they receive via the Receptions and Referrals Office and only use the Commission's database – if at all – when they need additional information (Respondents 1, 2, 5, 6, 7). Only one respondent reported primarily making use of the Commission's register (Respondent 4), while some also mentioned receiving information directly from Commission staff on an ad hoc basis (Respondents 1, 5).

Furthermore, as from 2006, all parliamentary committees had to designate one of their staff members as their comitology contact person, as did the Receptions and Referrals Office (Respondents 1 to 8). Some committees that deal with relatively many or heavy comitology issues (Economic Affairs, Environment and Transport) were able to hire an extra secretary because of this new assignment of responsibilities (Respondents 3, 5, 7).

It is worth noting at this point that the Parliament only adapted its internal organization following the introduction of stronger political oversight mechanisms by means of the regulatory procedure with scrutiny. A continuous flow of comitology documents to the Parliament had been high on its institutional wish list for decades, but its internal organization was incapable of effectively coping with the massive number of documents forwarded, leaving staff members looking for needles in a haystack until 2006. Only when new political rights were given to Parliament did the issue of document handling become pressing and were changes made (Respondent 5). This suggests that the need to organize information accessibly only arises when it is instrumental to a specific parliamentary right (in this case, the right to overturn committee opinions for which certain information is essential to have) as opposed to existing general rights such as controlling the executive by means of asking questions or making political statements.

Parliamentary committees differ extremely in the volume of comitology acts they can oversee. Four out of the European Parliament's 20 standing committees dealing with policy and budgetary matters have a particularly high workload with respect to this: Transport, Development, Agriculture and, especially, Environment (Respondents 3, 8). These committees, thus, have far more information to process than the remaining 16 committees.

Differences in information processing styles between the parliamentary committee secretariats are huge, as was revealed in interviews with three comitology administrators from the group of committees having a high workload. One of the administrators reported that he forwarded each and every package of information he receives from the Reception and Referrals Office directly to all MEPs in the committee. He also adds an abstract of the files attached and an internal deadline before which MEPs are to let the secretariat know they would like to discuss in committee whether or not they consider raising an objection (Respondent 2). In two other committees, which together work on the bulk of the RPS files and which – after alignment – will definitely be the champions of overseeing delegated acts, the packages of information are collected and forwarded together with a comitology 'newsletter' that includes a brief summary of the attached files (Respondents 5, 7, 8). In one committee, additional background information is provided about the issues by means of the newsletter (Respondent 5). These newsletters are released irregularly, but always between twice a week and every fortnight. This does mean that there is a slight time lag between the moment the European Parliament receives the information and the distribution of this via the newsletter, which eats away some of the time that the European Parliament has to adopt a resolution in the committee and in plenary. Nevertheless respondents indicate that in their committee this procedure was the most efficient, as it made it easier for MEPs to digest the information (Respondents 5, 7). In one other committee, the high volume of comitology acts has led some MEPs to voice a preference for not receiving all the emails. The secretariat staff has ignored such requests, regarding it as a political responsibility to select important files, not an administrative one, and hence has continued to ensure that all MEPs are forwarded all individual measures (Respondent 7).

The remainder of the committees also vary quite a bit in the way they oversee comitology decision-making. In one committee, all files are forwarded to all members of the committee (Respondent 4), but in another committee they are only sent to the coordinators of the political groups within the committee, together with a short background note (Respondent 6). One exceptional case has been noted in which the secretariat assumes a more active role. There the administrative staff filters out important RPS measures and forwards these to the chairman of the committee and the rapporteur of the co-decision act upon which the comitology measure is based, together with an assessment of what course of action would be most appropriate (Respondent 1). In none of the aforementioned committees, however, were newsletters produced.

Besides forwarding information to MEPs, the committees' comitology staff also informally network together in the 'comitology network'. This network was set up by the Co-decision and Conciliations Unit of the European Parliament, which on a horizontal level deals with interinstitutional decision-making. It meets several times a year and includes staff members of the political groups, as well as the comitology contact persons of the parliamentary committee secretariats. The network aims to be entirely functional for solving common practical problems, and to find common solutions or best practices with respect to keeping track of executive measures. Regarding the latter issue, topics that are discussed frequently are, for example, the changes introduced by the Lisbon Treaty, dealing with deadlines, and, interestingly, how to raise awareness among MEPs of the importance of comitology (Respondents 1, 3, 5, 6).

A parallel route for obtaining information on executive rule making in comitology committees runs via the general public. In the literature on parliamentary oversight this is referred to as 'fire alarm oversight'. It is generally seen as the more dominant form of information dissemination towards parliaments in the sense that it tends to receive more attention from parliamentarians (McCubbins and Schwartz, 1984). Fire alarm oversight with respect to comitology is facilitated through the online 'comitology register', an initiative of the Commission launched in the year 2003.[6] The online register is limited to documents actually sent to the European Parliament, and contains agendas, meeting summaries, draft measures, voting results and attendance lists.

The public register, however, is far from complete which severely affects the capacities of external parties to signal politically significant bits of decision-making to the European Parliament. A study of documents available for the year 2005 indicated that there is a huge discrepancy between the number of votes cast in the committees and the number of draft measures available: only 5.5 per cent of draft measures is available online (Brandsma, Curtin and Meijer, 2008). This means that the general public can obtain insight into how the committees voted, but not to which measures this voting relates. More recent studies into the online comitology register are not available, yet current visitors will still all too often find voting results without draft measures, summary records without attendance lists, only agendas or even no documentation at all for individual committee meetings. But even though the majority of summary records are available online – 67.8 per cent in the year 2005 – in many instances their quality is such that the reader will have a hard time figuring out what has actually been discussed in those meetings. About 85 per cent of all summary records are not particularly useful, not offering any information on the content of the discussions that have taken place.

When interpreting these findings it is important to remember that summary records and minutes are not the same. Summary records are meant to summarize the activities of the committee. These records are forwarded to the European Parliament and simultaneously made available online for the general public to inspect, or at least that is the idea. By contrast, minutes are classified documents, which are only available to the European Parliament on request, at the discretion of the Commission. Hence the European Parliament is not only handicapped in terms of the quality of the summary records it receives, it also cannot fully rely on external stakeholders to monitor comitology decision-making on their behalf. In the absence of greater public transparency of comitology, systematic organization of the admittedly vast amounts of documents forwarded by the Commission seems the only practical way forward. This has, in fact, been the organizational response of the European Parliament, as pointed out earlier in this chapter.

The European Parliament's sanctioning practices

In practice, the European Parliament makes very little use of its sanctioning instruments, and comitology matters are not often discussed in the parliamentary committees. Before 2010, only nine resolutions were adopted on the grounds of power abuse. The fact that any resolution of this kind was adopted at all may be surprising, given the fact that Parliament only has one month to adopt such resolutions in plenary, and that these are not binding. In fact, *droit de regard* resolutions only oblige the Commission to reconsider the measures in question, which means that it can get away with simply providing some further explanation on the contested measure (Lintner and Vaccari, 2009, p. 118). To the Commission, being the actor in this relationship, a *droit de regard* resolution is a particularly weak consequence, which it can, and does, safely ignore (Neuhold, 2008). In 2005 alone, the Commission's laxity in this respect led to its failure to forward any information to the Parliament on 50 adopted acts where the *droit de regard* applied (Bradley, 2008, 843–4; Lintner and Vaccari, 2009, p. 117; Neuhold, 2008).

Nor are other rights very often used. Until the summer of 2010, only three parliamentary vetoes were voiced on the basis of the regulatory procedure with scrutiny (Kaeding and Hardacre, 2010). Five further veto attempts failed in committee, and one final veto attempt was voted down in plenary by a very narrow margin (ibid.). The same patterns can be seen with respect to other courses of action, such as making political statements through resolutions. The Parliament's success with respect to body scanners was mentioned earlier (Hardacre and Damen, 2009), but only two further resolutions of this type were adopted between 1999 and 2005 (Lintner and Vaccari, 2009, p. 110). Only once has a veto threat alone made the Commission withdraw its measure, and a veto threat was used in only two instances as a bargaining chip for future legislative processes (Kaeding and Hardacre, 2010, 15).

Hence, the European Parliament imposes few to no consequences on the committees' behaviour. This may have many reasons, such as agreement with the adopted measure, but may also be due to parliamentary working structures hindering scrutiny, or a more general lack of awareness. Nonetheless, besides the dearth of consequences imposed, one might have expected to see comitology affairs discussed more often during committee meetings. A recent suggestion was that this might have to do with a lack of political interest in technical matters for which tight deadlines apply (Kaeding and Hardacre, 2010, 16). This concurs with the reading of respondents. According to an experienced official, before 2007 neither MEPs nor European Parliament officials cared about comitology at all (Respondent 3). But gradually, interest rose as a result of the new possibilities that the regulatory procedure with scrutiny brought to the European Parliament, and because the aforementioned 'comitology network' helped the committee administrators in their efforts to raise awareness.

There are still differences in interest between committees, though. One respondent complained that the information he circulates 'is evaporating', and that it is difficult to get MEPs mobilized and interested – especially when it concerns issues where the RPS does not apply. There are very few reactions to comitology documents, so that comitology issues are only rarely placed on the parliamentary committee's agenda (Respondent 2). One respondent even recalled a personal demand for help from a colleague in the support staff of another committee in finding tools to raise political interest (Respondent 1).

In other committees, MEPs do show more interest. One respondent indicated that in his committee, issues are discussed in the committee because the MEPs feel that the issues themselves are important. Only when they disapprove of a Commission measure do they start thinking about what procedure might be most fruitful. This generally ends up being a letter to the Commission instead of trying to express formal opposition, which is a time-consuming and uncertain effort and only has certain potential when the RPS applies (Respondent 5). Two further respondents observed that MEPs are most interested when RPS issues are concerned (Respondents 1 and 4); one of whom works for a committee that, in relative terms, deals with most RPS measures in the European Parliament (Respondent 1).

The European Parliament: A failing forum?

Within parliaments, attention tends to gravitate towards policymaking instead of towards controlling the activities of the executive (Andeweg, 2007). This is also true for the European Parliament (Maurer, 2007, p. 93–6), and for that reason the lack of interest on the part of MEPs may not be too surprising in itself. In most parliamentary committees, attention for comitology issues appears limited to those issues where the heaviest scrutiny procedure – the RPS – applies.

Having said that, however, the actual behaviour of the European Parliament on a day-to-day basis stands in sharp contrast to the never-ending quest for more control powers that has dominated the debate on comitology ever since the early 1960s. On that note one would expect MEPs to be very interested in matters over which it has fought to gain control for the past 50 years. There are two reasons why this discrepancy arises. The first is that the European Parliament's criticism against comitology relates to the set-up of the system itself. As Chapter 4 extensively elaborated, the European Parliament has always held the position that it should be on equal footing with the Council, and that the comitology system privileges the Council. In that regard the European Parliament has long felt that it was unable to scrutinize the executive effectively because comitology has long been, and to some extent still is, beyond its reach. However, this is a criticism that relates to the constitutional choices that underlie the system itself, whereas MEPs are exposed to policy choices that result from comitology on a day-to-day basis, and have to decide whether or not they need to take action, for example, by appointing a rapporteur and writing a resolution on a single policy file.

The second reason is that the Parliament's institutional position regarding comitology is prepared and voiced by three specific subgroups within the European Parliament: the legal service and the Legal and Constitutional Affairs Committees. When it comes to the day-to-day business of scrutinizing policies made via comitology, different actors are involved: policy committees such as the Environment, Agriculture or Transport committees, and the coordinating parliamentary services.

Although Parliament did not enjoy substantial specific scrutiny rights until 2006, it has always had means of controlling comitology at its disposal. From the interviews, however, it appears as if Parliament was waiting for these extra scrutiny rights before systematically beginning to process incoming information. Not until then did information on comitology become more accessibly organized, were dedicated staff members employed, and did the police-patrol-type control system begin working towards its full potential. But it remains questionable whether the somewhat higher interest of MEPs in RPS measures is in fact the result of the stronger oversight procedure in combination with police-patrol oversight, or rather of the stronger oversight procedure with fire alarms functioning as triggers.

As the previous empirics show, overseeing comitology measures on a day-to-day basis is a daunting task, and for many committees it is too much for MEPs to handle all on a structural basis. On this note, it seems plausible that MEPs in practice rely on fire alarms, which by definition are of a more accidental nature (Türk, 2003). But probably only true insiders can trigger fire alarms in a useful way, as even actual stakeholders may find themselves short of information. The information on comitology that is publicly available on the Internet reflects too little of the discussions in the comitology committees, both in terms of quantity and quality (Brandsma, Curtin and Meijer, 2008, 836–8).

Conclusion: Strong actors, weak forum

On the level of the committees, we see both strengths and weaknesses in the actual operation of the accountability arrangements. From a checks and balances perspective, it has already been noted that the current picture of accountability is not as bleak as it used to be in the early days of the committee system. Practices from the committees themselves show that comitology's actual operation provides for an even closer intertwining of member state and Commission officials than formally envisaged, thus strengthening the checks and balances in place on that side of the picture.

The relationship between comitology and the European Parliament, however, has both strengths and weaknesses from this perspective. Also, the strengths and weaknesses from a popular control perspective, which is also relevant to this particular relationship, are more or less the same. The European Parliament has seen its powers increase and receives all the information it needs for taking political action. This political action, in turn, can go beyond making a legality check or expressing vetoes in case of delegated legislation. Several cases in the past have shown that the Commission is, at times, also responsive to political messages made for different reasons in areas where the European Parliament does not have a veto right.

The weaknesses in this relationship are located both on the side of the actor as well as on the side of the forum. On the actor's side, two weaknesses are still the lack of public transparency of much of the committees' workings, as well as the lack of information contained in the summary records that are sent to the European Parliament. The European Parliament, acting as the forum in this accountability relationship, now has a system of distributing and screening information that potentially covers all incoming comitology documents, but its cumbersome internal procedures for adopting resolutions as well as its lack of interest in comitology issues per se stand out as obstacles to accountability. This results in accountability by accident rather than by design – not only in the case of opposition to RPS measures as concluded by Kaeding and Hardacre (2010, 9) but also across the board.

It remains to be seen if the changes emanating from the Lisbon reforms also result in different practices in this regard, but this seems rather unlikely given that Parliament's scrutiny of delegated legislation in terms of its internal procedures are very closely modelled on its existing procedures under the regulatory procedure with scrutiny. In fact, for delegated acts the European Parliament may even find itself short of information again, because the information regime as agreed with the Commission only has an informal basis and relates to the disclosure of information produced by expert groups, which also operate informally.

The accountability relationship between the European Parliament and comitology offers plenty of opportunities. The European Parliament's experience with its role as an accountability forum so far does, however, show a promising potential, which for the greater part remains under-explored by it. At the same time, the close cooperation between member states and the Commission continues to work at full speed, just as it always has. Now that the European Parliament's Constitutional and Legal Affairs committees have managed to negotiate formal information rights and scrutiny powers, part of the focus has to shift towards the internal workings of the European Parliament itself. Given the workload of comitology itself and the already high workload of the European Parliament in legislative procedures, carrying out improvements here is a challenge in its own right.

6
Participant-Level Accountability: Substantive Talks and Deafening Silence

Introduction

The previous two chapters on system-level and committee-level accountability addressed both the accountability relationships as envisaged in the design of the comitology system, as well as the actual practices in this respect. The core features of the system are that it is meant to provide Council (or rather member state) control over the Commission's executive activities, and that the European Parliament has gradually won ground in scrutinizing the decision-making that takes place within the committees. In practice we see that the committees indeed countervail the Commission's powers, which can mainly be concluded from the various interaction patterns of the Commission and the member state representatives in the committees. In a material sense, this results in joint decision-making of the Commission and the committees together rather than 'plain' committee approval or disapproval of the Commission's position without any room for reshaping the Commission's proposed policies. This is also the reason why the European Parliament has criticized the set-up of the comitology system over the past decades: it sees the committees as means through which the member states curb the Parliament's competences to scrutinize the executive.

At the root of all this is that the basis of interaction between the committees and the Commission is national interest. National interest may manifest itself in myriad forms, such as bargaining for policies that would be preferred in national politics, or seeking a solution that in a technical sense best fits existing national rules. On all accounts, some form of member state representation is central to the design of the comitology system since the committee participants formally give input on behalf of their respective member states.

This chapter, as the last of three empirical chapters, closes in on this part of the multi-level analytical framework. To what degree are individual participants in a collective decision-making setting, which also includes a supranational component, held accountable for the input they deliver to its deliberations? How do the member state representatives structure their input, and in what form is accountability rendered? To answer these questions, this chapter makes use both of survey material and interviews. Next to the survey sent to committee members, referred to in the previous chapter, which contained questions relating to the accountability of input given in committee meetings, a further survey was held, in line with the principal–agent model for analysis of accountability, among their superiors in order to capture the other side of their accountability relationship. In addition, interviews were conducted with a number of committee members and their superiors in order to gain a better understanding of the choices that are made in the daily operation of the accountability arrangement at the national level.

Discretion of committee participants

Before delving into the question as to what degree comitology committee participants are individually accountable for the input they give in the committee meetings, it must first be established whether they actually have any discretionary space to begin with. Do committee participants have room for manoeuvre, or do they merely read out positions written by their home departments? The deliberative image of comitology that was found to prevail in many of the committees (see Chapter 5) implies that committee members in general must enjoy quite some room for manoeuvre. The literature on comitology has put forward a range of different indicators that gauge various aspects of attitudes and behaviour of individual committee participants. These include role orientations and socialization, voting instructions and styles of representation.

Role orientations and socialization

There have been quite a number of studies into role orientations and socialization of European decision-makers since the late 1990s. Within almost a decade, an impressive body of literature has emerged on these matters tailored to, for instance, Commission officials (Hooghe, 1999, 2005; Checkel, 2005), but there are also many studies that pay specific attention to the socialization, roles and identities of committee participants (Beyers and Dierickx, 1998; Egeberg, 1999; Trondal,

2002; Egeberg, Schäfer and Trondal, 2003; Beyers and Trondal, 2004). Without exception, these studies indicate that committee members hold multiple identities at the same time, and mix them to varying degrees. Typically, such identities include national and supranational identities. 'Supranational identities' (or supranational roles) refer to an internalization of European norms that leads committee participants to display a willingness to pursue the common European good, transcending national interest (Quaglia, De Francesco and Radaelli, 2008, 157).

Such supranational identities do not completely replace original, 'national' identities; rather, they are complementary and are secondary to identities evoked in national institutions (Egeberg, 1999, 470–1). In this regard, survey findings stating that 34 per cent of committee members take the position he or she finds best on the basis of his or her professional expertise, and that 60 per cent feel a great degree of allegiance to their own professional background and expertise, or that 26 per cent believe that their colleagues from other member states act as either independent experts or have a mixed role between government representative and independent expert (Egeberg, Schäfer and Trondal, 2003, 32) should not be seen as discrepant but rather as indicative of role-mixing on a day-to-day basis.

But national identities themselves can also have a multitude of meanings. Observational evidence shows that a whole array of different things can be meant by 'a national position'. This can in fact follow from official departmental instructions, but can also be created by the committee participant himself following consultations with a variety of stakeholders that subsequently condense into a position that the committee participant himself refers to as the 'national position'. What is said to be a national position can therefore in reality be a departmental position, a unit position, a coordinated position between stakeholders or even an individual position (Geuijen et al., 2008, p. 85–102).

At first sight, both types of identities seem to correspond well with the two perspectives on accountability and how these have been fleshed into the fabric of the comitology system. From a popular control perspective, the comitology system serves to make sure that the Commission acts according to the interests of the institutions that endowed it with delegated rule-making capacities. The primacy of national role orientations fits this image of comitology. Supranational identities, in turn, apparently fit well in a checks and balances perspective in which the committees are areas of mutual dependence between the Commission and the member states, and where expertise-driven deliberation is the main mode of reaching agreement. The emergence of such identities, in fact, is one of the main indicators why Joerges and Neyer (1997a, b) saw comitology as a manifestation of deliberative supranationalism.

But despite the apparent fit between these role patterns and the two perspectives on accountability, these cannot be meaningfully coupled, since one relates to a property of individuals regarding their own behaviour, whereas the other refers to a characterization of the collective. This relates to the different levels of aggregation, as discussed at length in Chapter 2. Paradoxically, perhaps, the jurisdictional difference between the national and supranational level also makes different types of behaviour at the individual level relevant to the two perspectives of accountability. In this regard, the popular control perspective is easiest to apprehend, since the logic of delegation and accountability in this model implies that committee participants representing the member states must be accountable to a forum that is located within the domestic chain of delegation. Yet the exact same reasoning applies for the checks and balances perspective. Viewing comitology as a system through which member states and the Commission are made mutually dependent presupposes that member state representatives in fact do represent their home governments and are accountable to them. This reasoning is even part of the normative perspective of deliberative supranationalism, which stresses that the taking into account of the interests of different member states as opposed to the promotion of the interests of individual member states is key to legitimate decision-making (Joerges and Neyer, 1997a, 293; Joerges, 2006, 789). Thus domestic accountability and expert-driven deliberation go hand in hand in this model. Both types of role orientation may equally well fit the checks and balances perspective as long as there is a linkage mechanism to the national interest. Moreover, since member state representatives can apparently mix national and supranational attitudes, role orientation would not seem to be a very suitable indicator for the purposes of this study.

Voting instructions

The degree to which committee members receive voting instructions, too, does not completely gauge their discretionary space. A voting instruction may leave ample room for manoeuvre, especially when an accompanying negotiation mandate is formulated in vague terms, or when the voting instruction has, in fact, been prepared by the committee member him- or herself and subsequently rubber-stamped via the appropriate procedures. Still, the number of cases where such instructions are completely absent is informative. Several studies, each with different sampling strategies, show that about half of the committee participants do not receive clear instructions about the position they should take (Joerges and Neyer, 1997b, 613–21; Egeberg, Schäfer and Trondal, 2003, 36). The survey held among the full population of Dutch and Danish committee participants, as presented in Chapter 5, also included several questions in this respect. This showed that 46.7 per cent receive no negotiation mandate before a vote takes place in committee, while a further 8.6 per cent make and approve their own instructions. This leaves 44.7 per cent acting on the basis of instructions that are made and approved by someone else, in most cases being the direct hierarchical superior (Brandsma, 2010b, p. 245–7). But this indicator, too, only covers part of the discretionary space of member state representatives. Discussions taking place in committee well before a vote is taken, as well as the input given in the committees' deliberations, were not included in this measure, nor were less formal ways of instructing member state experts.

Style of representation

Another measure of how comitology participants in practice deal with their role as member state representatives is the degree to which they autonomously decide on the national position to be defended in the committees. This harks back to the notion that representatives employ different styles of representing a certain interest. In this regard, inspired by the work of Edmund Burke, Eulau et al. (1959) distinguish between focus and style of representation. 'Focus', according to Eulau et al., indicates *what* is represented: either the principal's interest or an interest which is defined otherwise.[1] In the case of civil servants attending comitology committees, this would be the national interest or any interest which is not necessarily national in kind, ranging from European supranational interests to technically optimal decision-making. Hence, focus of representation goes together very well with the different role orientations that have been identified and presented at the beginning of this section. But the 'style' of representation refers to something different, namely the degree of autonomy by which this interest is represented. Here, the question is: do committee participants act on the basis of formal or informal instructions externally imposed on them by their principals, or do they work on the basis of their 'unbiased opinion', 'mature judgement' or 'enlightened conscience'? In the former case, they act as *delegates*, in the latter as *trustees* – regardless of the question of which interest they are actually defending. The behaviour of delegates is constrained, whereas trustees are merely selected and thereafter are able to set their own agenda.

Obviously the two are extreme ends on a continuum of autonomy, but the distinction is useful for heuristic purposes. The literature is sparse regarding the question of whether committee participants generally act more as trustees or as delegates. In some studies, representation in committees is all about delegation (e.g. Steunenberg, Koboldt and Schmidtchen, 1996; Franchino, 2000a), in which case the presence of instructions is in fact all that matters for defining a discretionary space. Others have revealed considerable autonomy for member state representatives (Joerges and Neyer, 1997b; Weiler, 1999; Geuijen et al., 2008), while others again show that both interpretations may be applicable to some extent (Egeberg, Schäfer and Trondal, 2003; Pollack, 2003a; Krapohl and Zurek, 2006). For this reason, the survey among Dutch and Danish committee members also included two items on the style of representation, to which the respondents could express their level of agreement on a five-point scale: (1) I take the position in my committee that I think is best according to my own professional judgement, and (2) In reality I have considerable freedom to decide the national position in my committee. These two items were combined in an index measuring style of representation, or perhaps more accurately, degree of trusteeship (Chronbach's Alpha value 0.55). Table 6.1 displays the descriptive statistics of these variables.

The correlation of the trusteeship scale with the indicator measuring the presence of a negotiation mandate (see the aforesaid) is moderately strong ($r = -0.31$) but highly significant. This shows that this measure does relate to the availability of negotiation mandates, but also that this does not eat away all the variance. Some of this discrepancy can also be

Table 6.1 Style of representation

	Mean	Standard Deviation
I take the position in my committee that I think is best according to my own professional judgement	4.00	0.876
In reality I have considerable freedom to decide the national position in my committee	3.71	1.175
2-item scale of trusteeship (Chronbach's alpha: 0.55)*	3.85	0.873

* For additive index of items mentioned earlier.

seen in Table 6.1. Whereas the percentage of committee participants not having negotiation mandates, or setting their own, is around the 55 per cent mark, the mean of the index of trusteeship appears quite high.

In short, whatever their specific advantages and shortcomings, the indicators as used in the literature have in common that they reveal quite some discretion over input in committee meetings by member state representatives. Since both the popular control as well as the checks and balances perspective on multi-level accountability assume that a mechanism is in place that ensures that member state representatives in fact act in line with national preferences, this only adds to the relevance of accountability of participants in multi-level governance settings to their domestic principals.

Accountability of committee participants

Despite the relevance of accountability within member states for the input given in comitology committee meetings, this matter has hardly been touched upon in previous research. Although all the research referred to previously have been conducted at the *participant level* of comitology, accountability was never part of the discussion. Speculations, however, abound. Schäfer (2000, p. 23), for example, states that '[t]he awareness on the part of the representatives, both from the Community and the Member State level, that they may be held directly accountable for their decisions would be likely to affect their actions'. Larsson (2003b, p. 157, 169–70) poses the question whether we now have 'civil servants who are the politician's masters' as opposed to 'civil servants being accountable to elected politicians', while others argue that the partial disjointing of national allegiances found among committee participants challenges domestic politico-administrative relationships (Dehousse, 2003, 799; Larsson and Trondal, 2005). These expectations are well in line with more general analyses of the accountability of multi-level governance settings, which point to a dilution of responsibilities that may well take place given that individual member state participants can never be in full control over the eventual collective outcome (Oliver, 2009, p. 13–14; Papadopoulos, 2010, 1033–9). But can these claims in fact be substantiated? To what degree are comitology committee members in practice held accountable for the input they deliver in committee meetings?

The final sections of this chapter present empirical information on the workings of the final link in the 'chain of delegation' from the national parliament via ministers to civil servants, which is the first in the chain of accountability: from the committee participants to their immediate superiors. This final link has been selected on purpose. It is impossible for ministers, parliaments or chief executives to know everything there is to know, and therefore it is obvious that information is filtered out on the way from committee participants to higher echelons. Since those who are close to where the actual work is being done are likely to be better informed than those who have broader concerns, the focus is on the final link in the chain.

Data and methods

In order to gauge the accountability of committee participants towards their hierarchical superiors, data was collected by two different means: questionnaires and interviews. Actually two separate questionnaires were used. The first was the questionnaire sent to all Dutch and Danish committee participants, which has already been referred to on several occasions in this book (see Chapter 5). This questionnaire also included questions on the degree to which the committee members informed their superiors and others about the activities of comitology committees, including the input they gave in the meetings. As a follow-up to this questionnaire, a second survey was held among the hierarchical superiors of the committee members who took part in the first survey. For Denmark, a list of superiors was provided by Aarhus University on the basis of publicly accessible government staff registers.[2] For the Netherlands, the members who had completed the first survey were asked by email who their actual superior was.[3] In 225 active committees and two countries, 358 questionnaires were sent out to committee members and 294 were returned, yielding a response rate of 82 per cent for this group. To the superiors, 261 questionnaires were sent out and 153 were returned. This yielded a response rate of 58.6 per cent for the superiors. Both surveys together cover 34 per cent of all possible accountability relationships in the population.

Furthermore, eight semi-structured *interviews* were conducted with committee participants and 16 with superiors. The results have been incorporated in this chapter in order to validate and further substantiate the survey results. All but one of the interviewed superiors held the position of head of unit. Interviews were conducted both in Denmark and in the Netherlands. Interviews with committee participants are referred to in the text by the letters CP and with superiors by the letter S.

Denmark and the Netherlands were selected because their institutional make-up comes closest to the ideal-typical model of a single chain of delegation (and thus also a single chain of accountability).

The purpose of this analysis is not to compare the findings between these two countries. Rather, the aim is to collect and analyse the evidence from both countries and to discuss the implications of these findings more generically – hence the choice for two similar cases that have optimal conditions for accountability. The reason for including two similar countries instead of only one was to reduce the effect of possible non-response biases. Because there are two parties in each accountability relationship, both need to be investigated, and the risk of non-response is twice as great than if only one were to participate. Hence, two countries were selected in order to cover a sufficient number of accountability relationships for the analysis. Country-specific differences between Denmark and the Netherlands were controlled for, but were not found.

The scope of accountability relationships to which the conclusions of this analysis apply, however, may well go beyond those in unitary parliamentary democracies. Hierarchical accountability relationships are not unique to those systems, and in this respect the results of the analysis are also applicable to accountability relationships in federal systems such as Belgium, Germany and Spain. But for those countries, it is more difficult to ascertain to what extent flaws in one link of the chain of accountability also affect other links. The Dutch and Danish cases thus present optimal conditions for accountability.

Information: Active actors and passive forums

In terms of information, the superiors of the committee participants need to know about more than just their subordinate's contribution to the committee's deliberations. As comitology produces collective outcomes on the basis of interaction between the Commission and the member states, and the member states among each other, the superiors of the committee participants also need to know about the context of the meetings in order to know if certain input might have been feasible to secure. Without this knowledge, they lack an overview of the international field of influence and are thus unable to judge the behaviour of their agents. This means that they need to be aware of the input of the participant, but also of the content of the committee discussions, and the eventual outcome: the result of the vote. This yields three relevant subjects of information.

The surveys completed by the committee members and their superiors both contained a battery of three items on the kinds of information that are, respectively, sent or received: about the content of the discussion in Brussels, about the vote results and about the input of the committee member during the meeting. As it cannot be ruled out that a superior might come into possession of information via a third party rather than directly (McCubbins and Schwartz, 1984), this battery was repeated four times: one time each for information transferred directly from the committee member to his superior, to or from interest groups, to or from major companies in the sector, and, for the superiors, directly from the European Commission.

Table 6.2 clearly shows that the direct links are strongest. Committee participants were found to inform their superiors most often and vice

Table 6.2 Information received by hierarchical superiors

	Mean	Standard Deviation
From the committee participant		
Information on voting results	4.14	0.872
Information on the content of the discussion in Brussels	3.90	0.923
Information on the input of the committee participant	3.99	0.835
3-item scale of information from the committee participant (Chronbach's alpha: 0.90)*	4.01	0.796
From major companies in the sector		
Information on voting results	1.40	0.651
Information on the content of the discussion in Brussels	1.68	0.934
Information on the input of the committee participant	1.54	0.846
From interest groups		
Information on voting results	1.36	0.653
Information on the content of the discussion in Brussels	1.44	0.729
Information on the input of the committee participant	1.39	0.670
6-item scale of information from major companies in the sector and interest groups (Chronbach's Alpha: 0.92)*	1.46	0.638
From the European Commission		
Information on voting results	3.19	1.652
Information on the content of the discussion in Brussels	2.75	1.668
Information on the input of the committee participant	1.69	0.958
3-item scale of information from the European Commission (Chronbach's Alpha: 0.75)*	2.56	1.209

* For additive index of items mentioned before.
Note: All items are Likert scale statements to which the respondents could answer 'Never' (1), 'Seldom' (2), 'Now and then' (3), 'Often' (4) and 'Always' (5). Items were categorized using Principal component analysis with Varimax rotation and Kaiser normalization.

versa. The involvement of companies and interest groups appears to be limited. The committee members reported informing them less than their direct superiors; scores differ more than one full point on a five-point scale with those of the direct principals. But Table 6.2 shows that the superiors, in turn, were informed even less by these actors than by the committee members themselves. Here, a difference of over two full points was found. Moreover, the superiors of the committee participants regard information coming from external stakeholders as biased (S9, S11). The European Commission has an in-between position here. On average, it keeps the principals somewhat informed of the vote results, infrequently of the content of the discussion, and hardly ever of the committee participant's own input.

The figures in Table 6.2 do not mean that interest groups and companies are *always* less well informed by all committee members. The interview material shows clearly that providing information on committee proceedings is a matter of routine. All interviewed committee members who were asked this question indicated that they prepared a single document and sent it to several recipients. Such mailing lists can include both people within the organization and outside it (CP1, CP5). As one committee participant put it:

> We [committee participants] make the minutes. Officially I make it into a departmental memo, just by putting another header on it, and that is distributed to all interested parties that need to know about it.
> CP1

Informing people, thus, is done by carbon copy. The results of the survey confirm this: there is little variation in sending different sorts of information. This means that when an agent sends information on, say, the content of the discussion in Brussels to a recipient, he almost certainly also sends information about his own input and the vote results to the same recipient along with it. It also shows that those who inform their superiors to a certain extent do not by default inform all others to a *fixed* lesser extent. It can therefore be concluded that committee participants send the same information together in one batch, but to a variable number of recipients – depending on who is on the mailing list.

Despite the finding that committee participants generally do inform their superiors about their activities, it appears from the interviews that written reports very often go unread, or do not get much attention. Heads of unit and policy staff have a different span of control, and sometimes reading a report of a comitology committee meeting is simply not a priority:

> If you have something which is very politically sensitive or if there is a big important meeting you are preparing where ministers appear for the parliament [...] these items may consume all of your day. And therefore when this report from the committee meeting pops up on the inbox, you think, 'I'll read that later.' [...] Another situation might be that the report from the meeting comes in and it is a quiet day, and [...] you have not spoken to the committee participant for a number of days and is a good reason to call him.
>
> S1

> It happened that the international issues were put away because when the minister is calling you have to answer him, and Danish ministers are more nationally oriented than internationally. Because in Denmark he is going to lose his next election.
>
> S7

Most superiors indicated that they were quite satisfied with the information they receive. From the survey it appears that only 5.4 per cent of all superiors were unhappy with the information coming in; 11.4 per cent responded with a neutral answer; and, generally speaking, the remaining 83.2 per cent were satisfied. They were kept informed about the matters they wished to know and did not feel they were receiving too little information.

Also, they were found to tend to rely on the expert judgement of their staff. When superiors trust their committee participants to do the right thing, they are happy with receiving relatively little information (S8, S3, S11). This largely has to do with the aforementioned styles of representation. Trustees, or rather, those who superiors see as such, are simply not required to inform their superiors to the same degree as delegates are (Brandsma, 2010b, p. 68–74). The outcomes were different in two cases only: one superior said he always reads everything carefully (S4), and another felt policy specialists should behave less autonomously, but still only wanted to be informed of politically relevant things (S9).

The previous results show that the superiors are generally informed by the committee participants directly about the participant's own input in the comitology committee, about the content of the discussion in Brussels and about vote results. Of the superiors, 83 per cent reported being relatively satisfied with the amount and content of the information they received. But another, not particularly encouraging, finding is that this information is in fact not always read. In itself, it is not too disturbing that information gets lost *as such* – it is impossible for ministers, government, parliament or voters to be aware of every detail of what is going on anyway. But what these findings do show is that committee participants cannot simply assume that their superiors are made aware of certain matters merely because they are sent information about these on paper. The filtering out of information is not only due to conscious decisions, but also to less diligent and selective reading on the part of the principal, who has to cope with a high workload and to perceptions of heads of unit about the attitude of their unit staff towards their work that lie at the heart of their working relationship in general.

Discussions: Substantive talks and deafening silence

Comitology is an ongoing process. It is rare that issues discussed in a committee meeting are unrelated to other issues, or that issues that suddenly emerge in a meeting are instantly followed by a vote (Alfé, Brandsma and Christiansen, 2009, p. 145). Rather, backstage Europe is repetitive. Issues are repeatedly discussed, and policy proposals are repeatedly changed, until the Commission is confident enough of the committee voting in favour. During this process, member state representatives lobby the Commission to have proposals changed in a way that is favourable to them, but they also need time to find out the extent to which their home government can live with the policy alternatives that are discussed within the committee. This is why discussions, apart from evaluating past behaviour, simultaneously serve as a guidance tool for future input in decisions. Discussions can lead to new insights, new preferences and possibly also other input in committee meetings when the issue is again up for discussion. They serve as a means by which the committee participant knows if he is on the right track, and they equip the superior with a management tool.

Whether speaking of feedback discussions or of discussions in a more general sense, there are a very large variety of practices. This is a finding that emerges both from the survey and from the interviews. On a five-point scale from low to high discussion frequency, the average score of the committee participants and their superiors is 2.35. Discussions can also appear in various forms. Discussions can generally be the straightforward one-on-one meetings in the office (S1), but also unit meetings or phone calls late in the evening (S7), or simply popping in with a question or remark (S4, S6, S8, S13). Hence discussions tend to be a low-key affair. In some cases, frequent, organized feedback discussions involving a complete unit occur (CP4, S7), but there are also instances where hardly any discussion takes place at all (CP6).

Both the survey and the interviews show that the superiors of the committee participants are strongly guided by the information they receive. In the analysis of the survey results, a strong relationship was found between the degree of information provided on paper and the frequency with which committee affairs were discussed.[4] Providing information triggers further discussion, as several superiors also indicated in the interviews (S4, S1). Conversely superiors who endow their subordinates with a greater degree of autonomy also have fewer feedback discussions ex post, although these superiors are 'available upon request' (S11, S12, S13). This even applies in a rare occasion of agency loss:

> It has happened once that I said I was not happy with it, but we would try and make the best of it. Then, he found out too late that he was crossing the lines of his mandate. Things happen, and you don't need to make a big problem out of that. The alternative would be for us to prepare every single meeting together. Then I could just as well go myself.
>
> S11

Higher levels of autonomy granted to committee participants thus result in less information transferred to principals, and also in fewer discussions. As such this is not necessarily a bad thing. Delegates, who are entrusted with little autonomy, by definition act on the basis of their superior's specific instructions. In that case, the prime mechanism of accountability for superiors is simply to compare the realized outputs to the given instructions, and written reports, if necessary supplemented by additional clarification, suffice for this purpose in principle. But trustees set their own agenda, which necessitates different accountability practices. In their cases, the preferences of their principals are required neither to be explicit nor exogenous. Preferences can also be shaped in the interaction between principal and agent (Delreux, 2011, p. 45–52). What matters in the end is that the principal and agent share the same beliefs and act in the same interests. For trustees, the issue of information transfer to their superiors is therefore less relevant: it runs counter to the idea that trustees are supposed to act more autonomously. Yet in order to make sure that their behaviour is still in line with more general priorities, another adjustment mechanism is necessary: discussing principles on a more abstract level in order to align or realign the interests they defend. Discussions about core views and principles can fulfil this function, even if they take place irregularly (Brandsma, 2010b, p. 73–4).

This begs the question of what is actually being said in these discussions, irrespective of their frequency. Are they about fundamental points of view, and do they actually include an exchange of views? In terms of the intensity of discussions, practices are also varied as is shown in Table 6.3. In about half of the cases, these discussions are, to some or a greater extent, about basic ideas. In the other half of cases, the opposite applies.

Sometimes, such discussions simply do not take place because a situation is regarded to be *business as usual*. In that case, there is hardly any interaction between superior and committee participant: the issue was dealt with some time ago, and the organizational situation has not changed in the meantime:

> Whether I discuss extensively with my staff what should be said in a meeting or not, the basic idea we have will not be any different from last year's. And luckily we did not have too many staff moving on during the last years, so the people who ran the Council negotiations are now running the committee as well. So they are well up in this subject.
>
> S10

Many respondents believe that it makes no sense to revisit key principles time and again when an issue has been ongoing for some time already. Discussions – including political discussions – have happened before, and there is a group of people who have been working on the issue for several years. In other words, there is an established tradition

Table 6.3 Intensity of discussions

	Mean	Standard Deviation
The feedback discussions are about matters of principle	3.23	1.130
The feedback discussions are about the vision the (committee) spokesman has on the issue	3.36	0.961
The feedback discussions are about the vision the superior has about the issue	3.05	1.020
3-item scale of intensity of discussions (Chronbach's Alpha: 0.64)*	3.22	0.788

* For additive index of items mentioned before.
Note: All items are Likert scale statements to which the respondents could answer 'Always', 'Often', 'Now and then', 'Seldom', and 'Never'.

of behaviour upon which both the committee participant and the superior can fall back (Geuijen et al., 2008). In such situations, committee participants come to see their superiors when they believe something should be discussed, and, in turn, the superiors believe their subordinates only come to see them about the things the superior deems important (S2, S6, S10, S13, CP2, CP3, CP4, CP7).

Nevertheless, 'business as usual' can be problematic, as it underestimates potential future politicization of issues. Committee members may sometimes mistakenly think they can vote in favour of a certain proposal, when actually they simply cannot tell whether it is, in fact, business as usual. Several superiors refer to using cell phones and wireless Internet to keep in touch with the capital and to discuss certain items during the meeting, as an indication that this problem should not be blown out of proportion (S7, S8, S9). But in itself, this new technology does not solve the main issue. When new issues crop up under the guise of 'business as usual', participants are unlikely to contact their capitals at the outset:

> I have seen many times that people go for a practical solution, but after discussion in the capital they needed to move back. But often there is no way back.
>
> CP3

The interviews show that typically, superiors have a different understanding of political saliency from committee members. Committee members view the interest of ministers and parliament in the issue at hand as being salient; obviously, issues in which ministers, government and parliament have a keen interest are not intensively discussed between committee members and their superiors, as in such cases political preferences have already established and require no further debate (CP2, CP3, CP7). Superiors, on the other hand, tend to think otherwise, which results in different debating practices. They are not concerned by the extent to which their ministers are interested in a certain issue, but rather by how the interest of their ministers is distributed over different issues and the effect an issue might have on existing regulation. This is something that the survey does not measure, but which was disclosed in the interviews. This form of political interest does affect what the discussions are about:

> You have to make sure that [committee participants] have a political feeling. There are no straightforward solutions; it's always a balancing

act. You have to make it explicit that this balancing is political. If this understanding is lacking, people tend to make their own assessment of what people generally tend to agree on. And that is a very dangerous thing.

S11

Some things can be discussed [in Brussels] in such detail. For example, issue X can be about standards of what deviation from the norm is tolerated and what is not, and this tolerance can be different from the tolerance we apply now. And this could, for example, mean that a very large group of people that is now allowed to drive a car may suddenly not be allowed to drive a car any longer. This can land you in a lot of trouble [...] so you have to consider all points of view, and discuss this internally and see if the result is acceptable to [the hierarchy].

S9

Discussions can serve as a means by which committee members and their superiors – when necessary – can further clarify specific issues, or rather discuss core views and realign the interests they defend. But evidence so far shows that these discussions generally neither take place very often, nor are very intensive. Nonetheless, practices vary, and depending on their working relationship in terms of style of representation, one of these aspects may be more important than the other in order to ensure the accountability of member state representatives participating in committee meetings.

As an experienced committee participant said: 'In general you can say: we can do whatever we want to, as long as you can explain why you did something' (CP4). This may seem to be stating the obvious, but the evidence presented thus far tells a different story. Rephrased, this becomes: they can do whatever they want to, but often nobody asks them for their reasoning. The superiors of the committee participants are strongly guided by what information comes to their desks. This, in turn, also affects the discussion phase of accountability. The less information conveyed to the principal, the fewer discussions take place. Up to a point, this is not a problem. There is no inherent need for frequent debates with trustees; they are supposed to work autonomously, after all. But this role orientation does not relate to the intensity of discussions. Generally, these discussions are neither very intensive, nor very extensive. Mediocrity is what prevails in this respect. Ill-informed superiors are thus for the most part left asleep. Convinced that their agents are well-intentioned experts, they do not see this as a problem. And maybe, had there been a discussion, the superior would also have concluded that everything was fine. However, by hardly taking any interest at all, there is no way he could judge.

Civil servants work on the basis of tacit assumptions about the preferences of the minister and the Parliament. If Parliament has made its preferences explicit, all those involved know this and act accordingly. Comforting as this thought may be to some extent, this only applies to a minority of issues. Over 90 per cent of all committee participants indicated that political interest in their issues was tepid or less, with 22 per cent reporting that it was virtually non-existent. For the most part, people in comitology work on files that national politicians do not really care about, or they might not even be aware of them in the first place. Yet this is the same group that sets its stamp on 40 to 60 per cent of the rules, norms and other policies that are adopted by the European Commission (see Chapter 3), which do affect certain groups in society. And sometimes, superiors become aware that it is time for action. What makes them decide to do so, and how do they decide on what sort of measures to take?

Consequences: Carrots and sticks of accountability

Sanctions and rewards are the sticks and carrots by which principals can make agents comply with their preferences. These can involve anything from complimenting staff to firing them. In and of themselves, they are unilateral measures: forums impose them upon actors, and not the other way around. But whereas the 'observable' behaviour of sanctioning or rewarding is a one-way street, there must be something on the part of the actor, too, that allows it to have an effect. In a way, the instruments need to be credible to the actor.

There are two factors with respect to the consequences imposed by superiors: their repertoire of possible consequences, and the frequency with which they resort to using certain instruments. Some of these are formal in nature, such as the 'nuclear option' of dismissal or rewarding bonuses; others are more informal. The survey completed by the superiors revealed that nearly all had several formal instruments at their disposal to sanction or reward, such as redistributing tasks, firing staff or giving bonuses; these, however, are rarely used in practice – and not without reason. Giving someone notice, for example, comes with high transaction costs. As a head of unit mentioned, it shows 'you are really doing something wrong as a manager. It is an outright humiliation, let there be no misunderstanding about that' (S11). The decision to reallocate tasks, then, would seem easier and more credible to the staff (CP1, CP8). Sometimes heads of unit do this anyway to avoid tunnel vision among their staff. In that case, reallocation is less a sanction for specific behaviour than a more general management instrument (S12). But here too, superiors can have very practical motivations not to reallocate tasks, even in cases where they would prefer to do so:

> If it goes too far, this could mean someone is taken off a file. It is extreme, but possible. [...] But then, nobody may want to do the job instead. Because you have to read a lot and maybe also travel a lot, and there are only few colleagues who really enjoy that. Because you have to get up really early in the morning and you're home really late, or have to stay away for a night. These jobs are not always popular. And it's not always much fun to do. There are committees of which you think, 'Damn, I really don't like it.' This can be why sometimes jobs are not reallocated because the others would rather do without it themselves.
>
> S9

This does not mean that the job of participating in a committee is always the least preferred job in a unit. It is more a matter of finding the right jobs for the right people. Some subjects are easily mastered (S5, S7); in other cases, a particular specialist is needed to cover the European aspects of a particular issue (S3, S11). In such cases, a reallocation of tasks is not the most suitable instrument to steer future behaviour, even if a committee member does his job in a way that his superior is not particularly pleased with:

> This person really knows the ropes! He knows more about it than anybody else. I want to keep making use of that. And it would not be very motivating for someone to be moved to a less interesting file.
>
> S3

In short, the evidence shows that the formal instrument of dismissal is only used in exceptional circumstances. The transaction cost of using this instrument is high, and therefore it is not a credible option to policy specialists. Task reallocation is a more credible threat to policy staff. Here, too, the superiors of the committee members face transaction costs in applying this instrument. Individual committee participants may be indispensable in a certain position because of their expertise, or other people may not be interested in doing the job.

But whereas formal sanctioning instruments seem to be doing more harm than good, there is also a wide array of more subtle measures that superiors can resort to, which are also generally more effective:

> [Committee participant X] did a marvellous job. He drafted a new directive, convinced the Commission to adopt it, and shepherded it through the committee. So I gave him a bonus and took him out for dinner.
>
> S14

The bonus instrument this respondent refers to is one of many ways in which superiors can reward their staff. It also appears to be a well-established method of reward. Many heads of unit have a small budget available for bonuses, which is distributed among the staff in a certain predefined way. There are numerous criteria by which someone's performance is judged. According to the superiors it is 'very small money', usually about 1 per cent of the salary, but the staff members are very eager to get it (S1, S15, S16). For heads of unit, the trick is to find out what committee members *perceive* to be positive and negative incentives. This goes beyond a list of possible positive and negative formal incentives.

In any event, acting upon the behaviour of a committee participant shows that they are being watched. But being watched can also be experienced as a sanction in its own right. Closer supervision schemes can have a huge impact on the performance of individual people:

> Some people may find it dreadful that they are being supervised more closely and will go and look for another job.
>
> S9

> Especially thinking of [committee participant X], he is a person who can deal with bigger responsibilities. There is no better way of punishing him than to hold him on a leash. And that is exactly what you can tell him: you get the room for manoeuvre to do things, but in the confidence you are doing it well. If I find out things don't fit, this room will get smaller. So it's up to you.
>
> S11

Supporting someone in making a career move, or moving them into a dead-end career job, is a further step down this path. This is also a highly credible instrument in the eyes of committee participants (CP1).

And people can indeed be set back or promoted on the basis of committee activity:

> The guy who used to do committee X is our EU-coordinator now. He was doing an absolutely excellent job, he knew about *all* the files, coordinated everything [...] And then this vacancy came, and it was a true promotion, also in the sense that he got to a higher salary level.
>
> S3

Compared to the more formal incentives presented before, these results demonstrate that less formal incentives are considered to be more effective, and the instruments can be tailored to fit certain people.

Accountability in three dimensions

So far, the accountability of the comitology committee participants has been discussed separately with respect to information, discussion and consequences. But how accountable are committee participants on the whole? The accountability cube, as presented in Figure 6.1, will be used as a tool to present an answer to this (see also Brandsma and Schillemans, 2013). The elements of information transfer, discussion intensity and repertoire of consequences can each be scored ranging from 'low' to 'high'. This gives eight possible outcomes for the extent to which committee

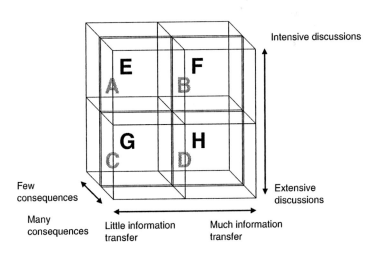

Figure 6.1 A three-dimensional accountability assessment tool

participants are held to account by their immediate superiors. Figure 6.1 shows these eight possible outcomes.

The eight outcomes shown in Figure 6.1 together constitute one three-dimensional space. Within this cube, the empirical results can be plotted at any point. The eight blocks within the accountability cube show in how many cases information transfer, discussion intensity and abilities to impose consequences are high or low; intensive or extensive, respectively; or few or many, and in which specific combination on the three dimensions the results occur.

Block C, for example, represents a situation of low accountability. The relationships between committee participants and their superiors that are found within this block are all characterized by relatively little information transfer, low discussion intensity and few opportunities of imposing consequences. In block F, by contrast, all elements are well developed. Relatively much information is transferred, discussions are intensive, and the superior is very much able to sanction or reward. The other blocks represent in-between situations.[5] Figure 6.2 displays the results of the survey by means of the accountability cube. No systematic differences were found between Danish and Dutch respondents.

The figure shows that the accountability block containing the least accountability (block C) is rather empty. Only 1.6 per cent of all results are found in this block. The other blocks at the rear of the cube are about equally empty. Only 6.3 per cent of all relationships appear to

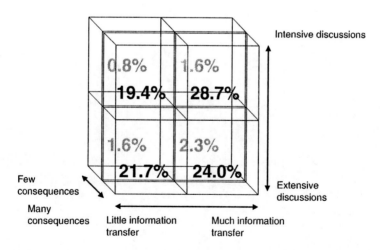

Figure 6.2 The accountability cube

contain three or fewer possibilities for making the committee member face consequences, either in a positive or in a negative way. This is hardly surprising, given the hierarchical setting. Nevertheless there are a small number of cases where a hierarchical superior is not in a position to compel the committee member to face consequences. This, though, is a result that is entirely based on the number of formal sanctioning options as captured by the survey. As the paragraph on consequences has shown, there are also many, subtler, ways of imposing consequences available. It is safe to conclude that, insofar as accountability is underdeveloped, this is not particularly due to lack of sanctioning or rewarding capacities.

Due to the difference in styles of representation between trustees and delegates, a proper accountability arrangement is defined by a large repertoire of sanctioning capacities, in combination with either a high degree of information or high discussion intensity. Situations where both elements are high could perhaps do with less of either of the two, but in any case these 28.7 per cent of cases are highly accountable according to all standards. In the accountability cube, appropriate regimes are thus found in block F, but also in blocks E and H. The remaining blocks are symptomatic of accountability deficits, which appear in 28 per cent of the cases. It would, however, be wrong to conclude that the remaining 72 per cent consist of appropriate accountability relationships. It must be kept in mind that situations E and H were deemed to apply to civil servants enjoying different extents of autonomy: delegates and trustees. Do blocks E and H, which contain essentially appropriate accountability regimes, actually apply to the right people? The results from the paragraphs on information and discussions suggest that they do so only to a limited extent. It follows from the analysis of discussions that there is no correlation between the content of these and the style of representation. The analysis of information shows that trusteeship indeed corresponds to lower degrees of information.

Further analysis confirms this. Taking into account the style of representation, defined as the role orientation which the superior likes his committee participant to employ, it appears that 33.3 per cent of the committee participants in block E are supposed to be trustees, while 50 per cent of those in block H are supposed to be delegates. From this point of view, 47.1 per cent of all committee participants are held to account to an appropriate degree.[6] In the remainder of cases, the relevant elements of accountability are shown in practice to be underdeveloped. In these cases, there may well be a risk of an accountability deficit.

Conclusion: Shirking actors or failing forums?

The set-up of the comitology system and the criticisms voiced by the European Parliament are all based on the premise that the participants in comitology committees who formally represent the member states, in practice also represent the national interest, for which they are held accountable in their respective domestic organizations. These committee members were indeed found to regard themselves primarily as representatives of the national interest (regardless of the question how they define this), although other, secondary role orientations may be in play at the same time. Moreover, in particular, about half of the committee participants receive no voting instructions, with a very considerable majority enjoying substantial freedom in organizing his or her own work. Compared to studies on the daily state of affairs in modern bureaucracies, this situation does not seem to differ from the way in which modern bureaucracies function in general (see, for example, Dunsire, 1978; Page and Jenkins, 2005). Participation in a comitology committee does not seem to induce substantially different behaviour than handling domestic issues does.

At individual participant level, this chapter has presented evidence on the extent to which comitology committee members are held to account at the national level for their input in committee meetings. All evidence indicates that generally there is no lack of sanctioning capacities at the disposal of the superiors of these committee members. However, in terms of information transfer, frequency of discussions and discussion intensity, cases can differ strongly. The study also shows that there is a tendency for committee members to look for prior political cues to relate their behaviour to. To a large extent, the observation here is that democratic accountability in this context has become supply-driven instead of demand-driven: the initiative for sending information lies with the committee member, and the superior may take this information both as a cue and as a basis for discussion. If scant information is transferred and behaviour goes undiscussed, superiors know little about the wheeling and dealing of their staff. A well-developed system for imposing consequences makes no difference in that respect.

This bodes poorly for the democratic accountability of comitology. This study has shown that in many instances, the immediate superiors of committee members do not keep track of their behaviour. Given the little public information that is available on committee matters (Türk, 2003; Brandsma, Curtin and Meijer, 2008), it is highly unlikely that higher management levels, let alone the minister, cabinet or parliament, are aware of the wheeling and dealing of comitology (Damgaard, 2000, p. 168; Larsson and Trondal, 2005). Yet neither can a properly functioning accountability regime, which has also been found in a significant number of instances, completely safeguard against agency losses. Further steps in the chain of accountability are needed before political actors or the public at large are reached (Lupia, 2006; Strøm, 2006).

Accountability towards superiors in the national politico-administrative system is important, both from a popular control as well as from a checks and balances perspective on accountability. In the popular control perspective, this is the natural result of the delegation of tasks from the public at large, via politicians, to civil servants. It is also vital in the checks and balances perspective, because the committees, at the European level, are installed as a means to balance the Commission's powers on the formal basis of representing member states. This presupposes accountability within national systems.

It is interesting to note that this study finds that the alleged shortcomings in the accountability of member state representatives, as suggested by several authors in the field, are actually found in other places than expected. Without exception, all point to the committee members who can, whether deliberately or otherwise, exploit shortcomings in domestic accountability arrangements that are ill equipped to deal with multi-level decision-making processes. This is said to take the form of blame-shifting (Papadopoulos, 2010, 1033–9), unawareness of any chances to be held accountable for their actions (Schäfer, 2000, p. 23) or secondary role orientations that challenge accountability relationships in the home organization (Dehousse, 2003; Larsson and Trondal, 2005). The findings of this study, however, point to yet another aspect of the functioning of accountability arrangements.

Given that committee members send many written reports to their superiors, it may be concluded that they are aware of the risk of being held accountable, and are perhaps even willing to render account per se. In fact, similar to the forum role of the European Parliament as analysed in Chapter 5, we see here that much of the actual functioning of the accountability arrangement depends on the behaviour of the forum rather than that of the actor. Even though the superiors of the committee participants are equipped with an extensive repertoire of means by which the behaviour of their subordinates can be influenced, be it formally or informally, they fall short in either systematically digesting the information they receive, or in making sure that they and their trustees prioritize the same interests in the policies handled by the latter.

For delegates and trustees, who enjoy different degrees in autonomy in doing their work, different accountability arrangements are appropriate, with respectively more emphasis on the transfer of information and the discussion of fundamental views. We see, however, in the empirical results, that for trustees, who are in the majority, not only is less information looked at by the superior, but that discussions are no more intensive than in other cases, and in about half of all cases, there may well be a risk of an accountability deficit.

In order to appreciate the full relevance of these findings at the national level, they should be understood in the context of the accountability of the comitology system as a whole. The previous two chapters presented evidence on the system and committee level of comitology, analysed from both perspectives on accountability. How does all this add up? The next and final chapter integrates these findings, and shows in this respect some remarkable strengths and weaknesses.

7
Comitology and Multi-Level Accountability

Introduction

Comitology is the European Union's most important mode of policy-making. Involving experts from the various member state civil services as well as those from the Commission, it not only produces the bulk of European decisions, directives and regulations, but also provides for a strongly organized space of interaction between officials working on the same policies within different jurisdictions. On the one hand, comitology has been depicted as a case of runaway bureaucracy. Several authors have pointed to its expertise-driven deliberations that make it hard to control politically (Dehousse, 2003), the lack of control powers of the European Parliament (Bradley, 1992, 1997) and the preference of the Council to, wherever possible, delegate broad decision-making powers to comitology, circumventing the involvement of the European Parliament (Héritier and Moury, 2011). These characterizations of comitology are well in line with the technocratic and even secretive character that is often attributed to multi-level governance settings in a more general sense (Oliver, 2009, p. 13–14; Papadopoulos, 2010, 1033–4).

But on the other hand, since the turn of the century several developments have taken place that seem to indicate that the problem may not be as grave today as it was in the past. The general trend across various European institutions is that they gradually become more accountable over time (Bovens, Curtin and 't Hart, 2010). A number of events show that this may well be the case for comitology, too. Although perhaps still not up to the highest standards, the transparency of comitology has, in fact, increased (Brandsma, Curtin and Meijer, 2008) and the constitutional fabric of comitology now also includes a much stronger position for the European Parliament (Blom-Hansen, 2011a, b).

So how accountable is the comitology system today? In the previous chapters, analyses of its accountability were presented on three different levels: the design of the system, the workings and accountability of the committees in practice, and the accountability of the comitology committee participants within their home organizations. This concluding chapter puts these findings together and assesses the accountability of comitology as a whole. After a brief recapitulation of the analytical framework used in this study, the chapter proceeds by filling this framework with the findings from the relevant levels of analysis, organized by the two main perspectives on accountability: popular control and checks and balances. They show that, apart from some outstanding issues, the overall situation is not all that bad. The findings bear an important message for those studying and assessing the democratic qualities of multi-level governance settings. In practice, the situation with respect to accountability may be much less dramatic than is often depicted, and also the risks and challenges for multi-level accountability may well be different from what is generally believed.

Multi-level governance and accountability

Accountability is part of the fabric of any democratic form of government. It has even been argued that it may well be its most essential component in a context where the vote of citizens is more inspired by rewarding or punishing past performance of governors rather than by prospective voting (Curtin, Mair and Papadopoulos, 2010, 930; Palumbo, 2010, p. xi). It is not exactly clear, to put it mildly, to which degree European governance can be said to be democratic, not least because the standards to which democracy should live up to in a European context are fundamentally contested (e.g. Follesdal and Hix, 2006; Moravcsik, 2002). But nearly all accounts stress the need for accountability to European and national electorates via the European Parliament, as well as via national governments.

But accountability is notoriously hard to organize when multiple organizations are involved, and especially when these are located at different jurisdictional layers. Accountability for collaborative intergovernmental decision-making may be relatively easy to organize when all parties are veto players, because under those circumstances a collective decision is a result of the consent of all parties. But things become more complex when some form of majority voting is the decision rule, rather than unanimity. Individual participants may be outvoted, so that their individual input, rather than the eventual output is the only thing they can realistically be held to account for. When, next to state actors, supranational actors also play a role in the decision-making process, the whole arrangement becomes even more complex.

Comitology may well be one of the most complex settings, since a variety of decision-makers at the national and supranational level have a stake in both its institutional set-up and its daily operation. Comitology produces supranational decisions that are adopted by the Commission, which also has the exclusive right to submit draft measures to the committees for approval. Comitology is meant to control executive decisions that further specify or apply legislation adopted by the European Parliament and Council. The latter two organizations decide on the rules of the game. Committee members, however, are affiliated neither to the European Parliament nor the Council, as they are policy specialists working for member states. They can, and in fact do, use comitology as a deliberative setting, which includes lobbying the Commission to adopt initiatives that take their own respective preferences on board. A myriad of delegation and accountability relationships is at play here at the same time, making it a challenge to disentangle who is held to account by whom and for what, or even to design a system of accountability that takes full account of all its intricacies.

It is striking to see that the legitimacy and accountability of comitology, as the most important multi-level governance process by far in the European Union, tend not to be understood in multi-level terms. The literature on these subjects is primarily focused on the institutional arrangements at the European level – with special attention paid to the position of the European Parliament (Bradley, 1992, 1997, 2008; Neuhold, 2001, 2008; Kaeding and Hardacré, 2010). On the whole, it ignores what may be required in operational terms and at different levels to make the system work. Comitology is multi-level governance in action; it involves a blend of different governmental layers, working together in a European setting. The member state level is even surprisingly absent in debates on the committees' legitimacy, even though the link between the member states and the Commission is their very raison d'être (Brandsma, 2010a, 491–2, 502–3).

Multi-level accountability

Multi-level governance settings also require multi-level systems of accountability. Chapter 3 reviewed the different purposes accountability may have, and examined the difficulties of analysing accountability for multi-level governance settings. Following Slaughter's approach of disaggregating sovereignty (2005, p. 62–4), but remodelling this to fit

148 *Controlling Comitology*

multi-level governance settings in full, a framework of analysis was developed that takes notice of all involved levels of decision-making, identifies the relevant actors and forums, and defines the objects of decision-making for which each actor can realistically be held to account. In this regard, the institution adopting the eventual decision is responsible for the collective product, and all contributors to the decision-making process are responsible for their own input into the decision-making process.

Figure 7.1 repeats the levels and accountability relationships that are at play here. Comitology is only one out of many multi-level governance settings to which this scheme can be applied. For the Open Method of Coordination, as well as for European agencies and their management boards, the framework as such is equally applicable in the case of different actors and forums. Comitology should therefore not be seen as an exceptional system in its complexity; rather, there are more such highly complex systems at work in present-day European decision-making. The workload of comitology, however, is quite exceptional with between 35 and 50 per cent of all Union measures being routed through it.

Figure 7.1 only shows the possible accountability relationships in the overall accountability-setting, but the relevance of each of the arrows in this diagram depends on the intended function of this accountability. This book identified two such functions: to achieve popular control,

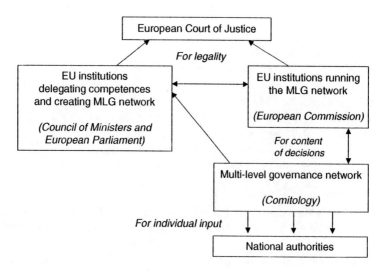

Figure 7.1 Multi-level accountability

and provide for checks and balances. From a popular control perspective, accountability is the natural mirror image of a delegation of powers or tasks, which in the end should result in feedback to electorates for decisions made down the line on the people's behalf. From this perspective the only relevant arrows in Figure 7.1 are those relating to feedback following delegation, namely towards the Council of Ministers and the European Parliament as the institutions who delegate executive tasks to the Commission and establish committees, and from the committee participants to their hierarchical superiors in their respective national organizations.

Seen from a checks and balances perspective, accountability is a means to ensure that institutions are constrained in their behaviour, in order to prevent tyranny of government. Hence eventual decisions must be able to be judged by an independent forum that took no part in the decision-making itself. This also implies that mutual dependencies are established through the day-to-day operations of an accountability relationship, so that no single institutions can dominate. In this regard, the arrows towards the Court of Justice are relevant, as well as the arrows to and from the Commission and the committees that may create mutual dependencies. Since the committees are established on the basis of national interest representation, which is the underlying type of interest that is meant to balance the Commission's powers in this set-up, the arrows from the individual committee participants to their own national constituencies are relevant as well.

The previous three chapters assessed the state of affairs with respect to the accountability of comitology at each of the three levels of analysis that structure the actual workings of the multi-level arrangement. In these chapters, the accountability relationships envisaged by the design of the comitology system were explored, as were the choices underlying the structures as these evolved over time. Practices at the committee level were mapped out, both in terms of the balancing potential of the committees versus the Commission, as well as the ways in which the European Parliament controls committee decision-making on a day-to-day basis. Finally, evidence collected at the national level was presented to show the degree to which committee members are held to account at the national level for the input they provide in the meetings.

In the end, how does all this evidence add up? On the basis of the complexity of the system and the accountability challenges arising in multi-level decision-making in general, the picture might be expected to be quite gloomy. Indeed, it has been argued that multi-level governance stretches and blurs lines of accountability, because individual actors cannot justifiably be held responsible for decisions that are not taken by unanimity (Strøm, Müller and Bergman, 2003, p. 744; Palumbo, 2010, p. xii). Others have maintained that, because of the technical matters that such settings usually deal with, committee members generally work 'below the radar' of their home constituencies, allegedly enabling them to exploit the lack of transparency of their decision-making setting to shift blame where necessary (Papadopoulos, 2010, 1033–4).

So, is it really all that bad? Comitology is the European Union's main executive governance mode. Between 45 and 60 per cent of all executive acts pass through it, which amounts to 35 to 50 per cent of all Union acts, and it has a multi-level set-up. Allegations on its lack of accountability have been many, and it has been subject of fierce interinstitutional rivalry, which, after the latest reform of the system, has still not been settled in full. Is there an accountability deficit here, and if so, where and how severe is it? Is comitology designed to be unaccountable? Is it truly a playground of policy specialists who simply cannot be controlled by any legislator at the national or European level? Or rather do all involved actors try to make the best of it, when it comes to reforming the comitology system and rendering account to the European Parliament or to hierarchical superiors in the home organizations of the committee participants? Let us therefore, through the lenses of popular control and checks and balances, look at the accountability of the comitology system in full.

A popular control perspective: Consistently increasing accountability

System-level accountability: Steady improvement over time

As seen from a popular control perspective, the accountability of comitology decision-making has consistently been on the rise, give or take a few ups and downs. The system at present primarily displays an accountability gap for implementing acts towards the legislative institutions. Historically, the committees were seen as instruments through which the Council could control the Commission in exercising its executive capacities. Before the European Parliament gained its co-decision powers, the picture was remarkably simple. The Council was the only institution delegating competences, and it could autonomously decide on control procedures and add these to basic legislation. In all cases, however, the Council itself only came into the picture after a sufficiently negative committee opinion. In all other cases, the Commission could go ahead and implement its policies.

It must be remembered at this point that the whole rationale behind installing committees of member state representatives in the early 1960s was to control the Commission while at the same time not overburdening the Council with work (Bergström, 2005, p. 48–53). In that regard, and also with a relatively small acquis at the time, the choice not to provide the Council with means to overturn positive committee opinions may not be surprising. But since in practice the committees behave as decision-makers in their own right, the missing link to the Council is no less relevant. In fact, when in 2006 the regulatory procedure with scrutiny was introduced as a functional equivalent to the delegated act regime, which at that time was postponed due to the failure of the constitutional treaty, the Council subsequently used its right of objection on six cases relating to the horizontal and politically sensitive issue of using correlation tables in transposition, while the committee itself voted in favour (Kaeding and Hardacre, 2010, 11).

The new regimes resulting from the split between delegated and implementing acts under the Lisbon Treaty Articles 290 and 291 (TFEU) have further increased Council control. Under the delegated act regime, control is placed directly in the hands of the Council, which may object to draft measures on any grounds. For implementing acts, the Council may object to a measure, adopted by the Commission following a comitology opinion, if it exceeds the executive powers conferred on the Commission. The latter right had not been asked for by the Council during the negotiations, but was agreed upon on the ground that the legislators needing to be on equal footing. From the viewpoint of the Council, the accountability of comitology as such has therefore consistently increased over time, despite the fact that it cannot overrule any decisions made pursuant to votes in implementing committees for other reasons than power abuse.

Developments regarding the position of the European Parliament are also significant. Until 2011, it has never been able to decide the rules of the game in a formal sense. During the legislative processes, it could only pick a procedure from the menu decided by the Council. Nevertheless, its position has gradually improved, first through inter-institutional agreements, later through arrangements made in the 1999 and 2006 Comitology Decisions. The right of scrutiny, allowing the Parliament to adopt non-binding resolutions on power abuse, albeit a right of very limited scope, enabled it to wield real clout. The regulatory procedure with scrutiny provided for much more extensive scrutiny rights than before. Rights to oversee individual decisions made under other procedures, however, remained absent. The current regimes on delegated and implementing acts reflect these developments. For delegated acts, the grounds for parliamentary objection have become unlimited, and for implementing acts the right of scrutiny lives on.

Currently, accountability is still incomplete, because of unclear arrangements for information transfer in the delegated acts system, and few possibilities for the legislators to impose consequences in the implementing acts regime. Nevertheless, over time the number and scope of accountability relationships to the institutions that are responsible for installing committees have grown consistently.

Committee-level accountability: System meets practice

In everyday practice, the Parliament is prone to behave more like a legislator than a controller. This is in itself hardly surprising, given that parliaments in general are more interested in making new legislation rather than scrutinizing the activities of the executive (Maurer, 2007, p. 93–6; Andeweg, 2007). With respect to comitology, this is evident in a number of respects.

First of all, despite earlier agreements on the transmission of comitology information from the Commission to the European Parliament, the Parliament only began to organize its internal methods for document handling in a systematic fashion from the moment it had succeeded in obtaining very specific political rights to oversee parts of the decision-making taking place in comitology committees. This also included appointing dedicated support staff for comitology affairs to every parliamentary committee, which is the location where control is exercised in practice. But even though such a structure is now in place, overseeing comitology measures on a day-to-day basis is a daunting task, if only because of the sheer volume of acts passing through it. For many committees, it is too much for MEPs all to handle on a structural basis (see Chapter 5). The information that is made publicly available via the Internet register of comitology, following the 2011 reform, only includes implementing committees and no information on the activities of delegated act expert groups, and is not of much help to interested parties who might work as fire alarms for the European Parliament (Brandsma, Curtin and Meijer, 2008).

Second, before any resolution can be adopted in plenary, drafts have to follow a time-consuming route mainly via committee meetings and coordinators meetings. These are not procedures that are specified in the Treaty or in any Comitology Decision, but that have resulted from the rules of procedure adopted by the European Parliament itself. Usually a one to four month deadline applies to adopting such a resolution, and plenary meetings take place only once a month. In this respect, the European Parliament has created its own obstacles to accountability. Having said that, it has in the recent past succeeded in getting some resolutions through plenary and tabling an additional number in committee. It has also succeeded a number of times in taking political action that went beyond making a legality check or vetoes in case of what is now referred to as delegated legislation, and at times the Commission has proved responsive to the Parliament's wishes. It may therefore be concluded that the European Parliament fails to exhaust in full the available opportunities, which in part may well relate to its own cumbersome internal working procedures.

Participant-level accountability: Trustees on the loose?

At the level of the individual participants to the comitology committees, we have seen that the committee members have a fair degree of autonomy over their own work. Whether measured by the degree to which they are equipped with instructions or by the degree to which they themselves report to be working autonomously, various earlier studies as well as the one presented in this volume point to considerable freedom on the part of the committee members. These indicators demonstrate that the committees' member state representatives in fact do have some room for manoeuvre, and hence they do have something to be accountable for. In fact, the relatively high degree to which they report back in writing to their superiors does display a general willingness to provide information on the goings on in the committee.

However, in similar vein to the findings on the side of the European Parliament, it has also been observed that hierarchical superiors, although generally happy with the amount and quality of the information coming in, find it hard to find the time to digest the incoming information. Other files often take priority, which results in comitology information landing on a pile of paper that, in the end, is never read. In their working relationship within their home organizations, committee participants are expected to function as trustees and accordingly perform their work autonomously. The domestic principals are happy receiving less information, and their trustees oblige by sending less. While more behavioural autonomy also leads to fewer discussions, the sending of written information independently fosters discussion. Yet in terms of the content and intensity of the discussions, this makes no difference. Discussions tend to be neither very frequent nor intensive. Opportunities for imposing consequences, however, are many, both in the form of formal and informal sanctions and rewards.

All in all, evidence at the national level shows that trustees are left alone to a much greater extent, after which superiors risk to lose sight.

Figure 7.2 next summarizes these findings. The strength of the accountability relationships is reflected by the thickness of the arrows. Dashed lines refer to the delegated acts regime, whereas full lines represent the implementing acts regime.

All in all, from a popular control perspective the news is not all bad. The system's design has provided for an ever-increasing level of accountability for comitology decision-making, but there is still a gap between the formal set-up of the system and the functioning of accountability on a day-to-day basis. In this regard, the position of the European Parliament position is especially remarkable. Over the last two decades, its role in the accountability of comitology has increasingly been brought in line with its formal legislative competences, although unlimited control for implementing acts still remains a bridge too far. Nevertheless, the whole system remains firmly built on the premise that the input of member state representatives in the committees is by default in line with any positions the Council might take on those matters. This, however, need not necessarily be the case, since this involves different people acting on the basis of different interests. Also, this premise assumes that there is accountability at the national level for the input that is given in the committees. While many committee members may certainly be held accountable for this, it does not hold true in all cases, especially due to the behaviour of the forums at this level. Interestingly, the same observation has been made with respect to the actual behaviour of the European Parliament. Due to its own cumbersome internal procedures for adopting resolutions, as well as its lack of interest in comitology issues per se, the Parliament fails to exhaust its

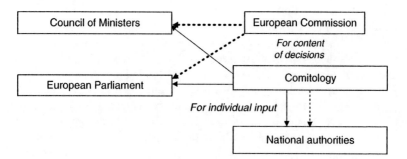

Figure 7.2 Comitology's multi-level accountability from a popular control perspective

capacities as an accountability forum, despite its own extensive information system on comitology matters (see Chapter 5; also Kaeding and Hardacre, 2010).

A checks and balances perspective: Success at risk

System-level accountability: Reverse point in sight?

When it comes to balancing the Commission's executive powers, there is no doubt that comitology must be seen as a remarkable success story. Because the voting procedures used in the committees produce consequences, the Commission is forced to cooperate with the member state representatives so that in the end comitology produces joint decisions. This has enabled the Commission to take account of the interests of member states and to create goodwill and compliance with the eventual policies. It also furnishes member states with the opportunity to give input to the Commission, in order to lobby for certain favourable policies. The voting rules thus force both the member states as well as the Commission into a cooperative mode.

We may ask whether this collaborative setting itself is not a power of its own that needs balancing in its own right. But here, the gradual involvement of the European Parliament comes into picture. Its powers, however, cannot compare to those of the member state representatives. Although it does, in fact, have veto powers and powers of revocation with respect to delegated acts, its powers of control over implementing acts remain non-binding and limited in scope. Nevertheless it has shown itself capable of exerting influence when necessary, by bargaining and adopting political statements in plenary. Since the European Parliament is a political actor by its very nature, unlike the member state representatives in the committee, the civil servants working for the Commission and the representatives of the member states working for the Council, all of whom are executive actors, it remains questionable whether innovations such as participation rights in the committees would really be any help for the European Parliament.

At the system level, the current set-up of the system provides for plenty of checks and balances in the sense that many actors are mutually dependent on one another for making a decision. However, there are certain signals that the future may not be too bright after all. In recent reforms, the Commission has adopted a minimalist approach to control (Blom-Hansen, 2011b, p. 53–94) resulting in a gradual erosion of the strength of the voting procedures. The 1999 Comitology Decision got rid of the 'contrefilet' or 'b' variants of the voting procedures, which stipulated that any matter forwarded to the Council should be suspended during the Council's deliberations and that, in case of the b-variant of the regulatory procedure, a simple majority of member states could block the Commission. From that time on, any blockade by the Council required an objection by a qualified majority within three months. Technically, this means that the Commission can get proposals adopted, even under the regulatory procedure, as long as no qualified majority of member states objects. When draft acts fail in the committee because a qualified majority in favour cannot be found, the Commission simply needs to wait for the Council to fail to object by a qualified majority. The 2011 reform shows that the Commission, in inter-institutional negotiations, very much prefers to curtail the committees' powers.

Throughout the history of comitology, strict procedures did not prevent the Commission from working together in harmony with the committee members. But as the rules of the game have evolved over time, the need for member state support in committee has steadily decreased with every reform. Moreover, in the 2011 reform, the Commission pushed strongly to weaken the voting procedures even further. Why would the Commission want the voting procedures to lose their 'bite', despite the (on the whole cooperative) style of decision-making in comitology? Why is it so keen on getting rid of the formal necessity to take into account possibly opposing interests before being able to move forward? Mutual dependence in a formal sense is slowly but surely evaporating in the fabric of the comitology system.

The same is true for delegated act committees, which are formally no longer required to approve of the Commission proposals as their votes, if any, have no binding consequences. Combined with strategic dissemination of information towards the Council and Parliament, this affords the Commission substantial freedom in practice, as these two legislative institutions are physically unable to devote full attention to all draft delegated acts in the first place. The fact that the Commission's practices on publishing information emanating from expert groups are in no way comparable to those of the old comitology regime, which in itself was not quite perfect (Brandsma, Curtin and Meijer, 2008), is an additional handicap to the Council and the European Parliament. Although the Council and the European Parliament enjoy more control powers with respect to delegated acts than previously under the regulatory procedure with scrutiny, in terms of checks and balances the new regime, at least from a systemic point of view, is a considerable step back.

Committee-level accountability: More than expected

As previously noted, the workings of the committee system may in practice differ from what might be expected on the basis of its formal set-up. The case investigated by Joerges and Neyer (1997a, b), which they used to support their normative framework of deliberative supranationalism may have been extreme, but overall the dominant interaction mode for decision-making in comitology committees would certainly seem to be deliberation. Furthermore, the Commission would appear to be quite accommodating with respect to the specific interests of member states that are not necessary for getting its proposals through. These two forms of behaviour within the committees are both indicative of a low level of confrontation between the Commission and the member states; in fact, more interests would appear to be taken into consideration than strictly necessary from a procedural point of view (Alfé, Brandsma and Christiansen, 2009). In fact, previous empirical research into the Commission's accommodating attitude during the committee meetings could not attribute this to the strength of the voting procedures used in the committees (Brandsma and Blom-Hansen, 2010). Ultimately, therefore, the gradual reform of committee procedures may not affect the countervailing powers of the committee system after all, if current practices continue.

It is exactly because of the, in practice, very close relationship between the Commission and member state representatives in the committees that comitology has been considered to be a decision-maker in its own right. The Commission and member state experts, who meet behind closed doors and only discuss matters that lie within their field of expertise, which more often than not are incomprehensible to outsiders, may easily be driven by a spirit of enthusiastically creating new policies together as opposed to controlling the executive capacities of the Commission (Dehousse, 2003). Although comitology may originally have been conceived of as a control device, concerns about the perils of administrative integration have been voiced since the 1960s, most notably by the European Parliament. In practice, it has to some degree become able to be a balancing power in its own right not only due to the specific rights that are laid down in the design of the comitology system, but also due to its own strategic use of co-decision powers. Where the European Parliament has veto powers, the Commission would be wise to consult the European Parliament informally before matters are put before the committees. Where it does not have such powers, the European Parliament can still make a difference by adopting non-binding resolutions. Nevertheless, experience has taught that particular matters, regarding which the European Parliament lacks comitology-specific veto powers, tend to attract very little interest, so that its full balancing potential remains under-exploited.

Participant-level accountability: Do participants represent member states?

At the level of committee participants, the main question from this perspective as well is the degree to which committee participants are accountable to a forum higher up the hierarchical ladders of their home organizations. But the function of this accountability relationship is somewhat different. Whereas from a popular control perspective the aim is to ensure that committee participants defend the national interest, from a checks and balances perspective the focus is shifted more towards the role of individual committee participants in the collective setting. Since the checks and balances in the comitology regime are partly based on member state representation, the question is whether domestic accountability arrangements are in line with this premise.

Proxies that tap into identities assumed by committee members in committee are not very helpful in this respect. The main problem is that the concept of 'member state representation' or 'representing the national interest' is an umbrella concept that is very hard, if not impossible, to gauge precisely. It is a concept that encompasses a host of different meanings, as was shown at length in Chapter 6. From the point of view of the committee participants, who always speak on behalf of their country in the committee meetings, they primarily represent the national interest.

In order to be more specific, this research has tapped into the degree of autonomy enjoyed by the committee participants, and the degree to which they are held to account for their input by their hierarchical superiors, who are the first in line to, if necessary, give a political mandate. Committee members enjoy a considerable degree of autonomy. In practice, the accountability regime does not always match this autonomy, as a result of which 'trustees' in particular become more vulnerable to being unaccountable in practice. From a checks and balances perspective, the consequences of these findings need to be put in the context of the accountability arrangement of comitology as a whole. Serious doubts may be raised as to what is actually being represented in the committees that serves to balance the Commission. It is doubtful that the participation in the committees is truly 'national' in the sense that political actors instruct and/or check their administrators in comitology committees. Although in earlier days the Council viewed management committees as a convenient solution to relieve the Council of work, it is highly questionable whether, hypothetically speaking, measures agreed by the member state representatives in comitology would also be agreed by Council members. After all, these are two wholly different organs that are in interaction with different actors and are part of different lines of accountability. The overturning by the Council of a number of measures adopted by committees working under the regulatory procedure with scrutiny is telling in this respect.

Figure 7.3 shows the multi-level accountability arrangement as seen from a checks and balances perspective. Again, the dashed lines refer to the delegated acts regime and the full lines represent the implementing acts regime, and the strength of the accountability relationships is reflected by the thickness of the arrows.

On the whole, practice has shown that the powers of the Commission are quite well constrained through comitology. These constraints emanate more from the attitude of the Commission in comitology meetings than from the strength of the voting procedures specified in the system's design. Even the European Parliament, which was considered to be a relative outsider for most of comitology's history, is able to join in this balancing exercise, in anticipation of a possible parliamentary veto under the delegated acts regime or the regulatory procedure with

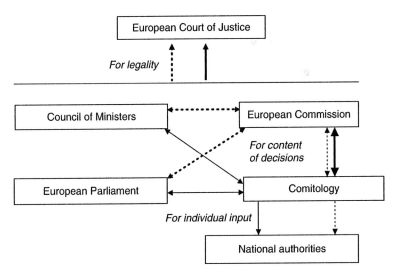

Figure 7.3 Comitology's multi-level accountability from a checks and balances perspective

scrutiny. Besides that, the Parliament has several political, non-binding instruments at its disposal. Only the accountability practices at the national level show that the Commission may be dependent on the behaviour of actors in a committee, which represent the interests of their national constituencies only in name.

Although all these practices seem well established, it is clear that the formal 'bite' of the committees has been diminished over time, and that the existence of the delegated act expert groups is only based on an informal agreement. These groups also lack formal powers to control the Commission: their opinions are not binding on the Commission per se. Still these delegated act expert groups are meant to be control devices also in the sense that they may trigger objections by the European Parliament and the Council through the information that is provided on their meetings. However, the overall arrangement for delegated act expert groups is of such a vague and non-binding nature that, ultimately, the European Parliament and the Council may well receive less information than they did in the past, which seriously undermines their capacity to balance the Commission's powers.

In comparison, the regimes of delegated acts and implementing acts in the comitology system should be evaluated differently. The same regimes can also be evaluated differently depending on the perspective on accountability used for evaluation. Table 7.1 brings these different evaluations together. It shows that the implementing acts system affords a very decent degree of accountability, both from a popular control and from a checks and balances perspective, despite the complexity of the current voting rules, and despite gaps in some national accountability relationships and in the degree to which the Council and the European Parliament can step in. Not least, it has proven to be remarkably well capable of balancing the Commission's powers, well beyond their formal powers.

The picture for the delegated acts regime is quite different. Here we see a very strong accountability design in terms of popular control, as both

Table 7.1 Three levels, two perspectives

	Popular control perspective	Checks and balances perspective
System level	+/– (implementing acts)	+ (implementing acts)
	++ (delegated acts)	+ (delegated acts)
Committee level	+/– (implementing acts)	++ (implementing acts)
	+/– (delegated acts)	– (delegated acts)
Participants level	+/– (both regimes)	+/– (both regimes)

legislative branches enjoy full scrutiny powers over the eventual decision. However, because these two branches face organizational problems in scrutinizing all delegated rule-making, they have to rely on information provided by the expert groups that have been designed as part of the system. These serve as signalling tools to the European Parliament and the Council, but have been established on an informal basis. Moreover, the dissemination of information from the expert groups to the Council and the European Parliament also occurs on an informal basis only. This offers plenty of escape routes for the Commission to evade control and use the informal agreements strategically. This is also part of the reason why, at the committee level, the regime is considered to be poor; furthermore, the committees themselves only give non-binding commitments, which removes the need for the Commission to engage in lengthy deliberations with the committees in order to make a joint decision.

Conclusion: New challenges of multi-level accountability

The overall picture shows that there is quite some room for improvement. But then again, the current situation is not as dramatic as one might be tempted to believe. The literature that addresses accountability with respect to multi-level governance settings paints a far too gloomy picture of its workings. Some previously identified obstacles hold true by definition, such as the assertion that accountability lines are stretched and blurred for issues that relate to European decision-making (Palumbo, 2010, p. xii), or that single participants cannot justifiably be held to account for a collective decision, if this should include a supranational component (Strøm, Müller and Bergman, 2003, p. 744). This, in practical terms, is said to encourage blame-shifting (Oliver, 2009, p. 13–14; Papadopoulos, 2010, 1033–4).

The arrangement surrounding comitology indeed shows that many actors and forums are at work here at the same time, but also that ways can be found of dealing with this complexity. The object for which account is rendered is tailored to the natural role of the forum in the overall institutional system and to the jurisdictional boundaries to which the accountability relationships are subject. This means that accountability for final decisions can, in fact, be located with a forum at the supranational level. What is left at the national level is accountability for the input provided to the committees' deliberations. On that note, it is much easier to shift the blame if the eventual decision is the object of accountability, rather than an actor's own input. The structure of accountability for the most important multi-level governance setting in the European Union is therefore not designed to exploit these obstacles to accountability in full, in order to avoid as far as possible having to render account. Instead, it allows all involved actors and forums to make the best of it, given their own natural spheres of competence.

Differences between set-up and practices

Nevertheless, the present analysis, made across the levels that make up the full arrangement, does highlight two factors that decisively affect the workings and quality of the accountability regime, which earlier research did not touch upon. The first is that the design of an accountability arrangement may well be different from its day-to-day functioning. The difference between *de jure* design and *de facto* operations has been noted in several studies on the functioning of comitology as such (Joerges and Neyer, 1997b; Brandsma and Blom-Hansen, 2010; Blom-Hansen, 2011a), but seems not to have made its way into studies of accountability (Bovens 2007a, b; Bovens, 't Hart and Schillemans, 2008). Formal provisions eventually materialize into practices, and should therefore be included when the functioning of an accountability regime is evaluated. These practices may of course well be the result of constitutional engineering, but they may also have come about informally and completely separately from the formal design of the system. The deliberative interaction mode in the committees and the accommodative attitude of the Commission both testify to the fact that such behaviour that did not follow from any formal agreement may be even more constraining to an actor than the formal agreement itself. By analogy, practices that take place as a result of formal rules may well be inconsistent or even hardly existent, making the formal regime effectively a dead letter. The European Parliament's, and now also the Council's, right to check the legality of comitology measures is an instrument that – due to the very narrow scope of objections, their non-binding character, very tight deadlines and cumbersome procedures – is so hard to use that it is often disregarded straight away.

The role of the accountability forum

A second factor highlighted in this study is that the actual functioning of the accountability relationship seems more dependent on the behaviour of the forum than on that of the actor. Whereas the committees themselves very actively interact with the Commission and balance its powers through deliberation and accommodation, the European Parliament and the domestic superiors of the committee participants employ inconsistent practices in order to hold their respective actors to account. Wherever these practices, despite formal structures of accountability, allow actors to work without constraint, we can speak of *failing forums*. The literature on accountability, and especially the segment that makes use of principal–agent models, primarily evaluates its functioning on the basis of the preferences of the agent, the preferences of the principal and accountability mechanism put in place by the principal. Under the assumption that agents will always try to find a way in which they can maximize their own preferences rather than those of their principals, accountability mechanisms are meant to deter agents from shirking so that their actual behaviour is more in line with the principal's expectations (Strøm, 2000, 2006; Lupia, 2006).

What practices in the European Parliament, as well as at the national level reveal, is that often the forums refrain from acting upon their actors' behaviour. This is not because they know that they agree with the position taken by them, but because of reasons that have no bearing on the content of the issue. They may be overburdened with other work, for instance, or procedures for imposing consequences may be too troublesome. Holding actors to account simply does not give them the pay-off they are after, or comes with transaction costs that are too high to be worthwhile. At the same time, paradoxically enough some of these transaction costs have come about by virtue of the behaviour of the forum itself. The lengthy and cumbersome procedures for adopting resolutions in the European Parliament, for instance, did not arise as the result of a Treaty obligation, but rather as the result of the European Parliament's own rules of procedure. While the relevant actors very properly send information to their forums, a number of these forums have responded by adopting a very passive attitude. Once the actors become aware of this, they may well pursue this advantage and the resulting 'agency loss' ensues from a failing forum.

Although accountability is generally seen as particularly hard to achieve in a multi-level setting of governance, this study has shown that comitology, as the most active multi-level policymaking process in the European Union, is definitely not as unaccountable as one might expect at first sight. Its design allows for accountability for the eventual decision, as well as for the input of each respective committee member. The objects in respect of which actors are to render account are neatly broken down along the different jurisdictional levels at which they are active. Control for legality is also safeguarded. Depending on the situation at hand, different actors and forums can be identified, both of whom should, in practice, make the most of the available opportunities.

In principle, numerous arrangements to make accountability work are already in place, and working, in some cases, at full speed. In practice, as this book has shown, several obstacles stand in the way of full accountability, and even though clearing these away may prove to be a challenge in its own right, this does not require making legislative or constitutional changes. Despite its shortcomings, the system may thus well serve as a convenient template for the accountability of other 'new' modes of multi-level governance.

Annex: Overview of Sources Regarding the Post-Lisbon Negotiations on Comitology

Official documents:

- Report by the Council Presidency to the European Council on preparatory work in view of the entry into force of the Lisbon Treaty (Council 2009a)
- Report by the Presidency to COREPER on the implementation of Articles 290 and 291 TFEU (Council 2009b)
- Introductory note by the Presidency to COREPER II on the implementation of Articles 290 and 291 TFEU (Council 2009c)
- Report from the Friends of the Presidency Group to COREPER II (Council 2010a)
- Communication from the Commission on the implementation of Article 290 TFEU (Commission 2009b)
- Commission proposal for a regulation laying down the rules and general principles concerning mechanisms for control by member states of the Commission's exercise of implementing powers (Commission 2010c)
- Note a l'attention des members du GRI (Commission 2010d)
- European Parliament resolution of 7 May 2009 on Parliament's new role and responsibilities in implementing the Treaty of Lisbon (European Parliament 2009a)
- European Parliament Draft report on the power of legislative delegation (European Parliament 2010a)
- European Parliament Report on the power of legislative delegation (European Parliament 2010b)
- Minutes of the Committee on Legal Affairs, 2 September 2010 (European Parliament 2010c)
- European Parliament Draft report on the proposal for a regulation on control by member states on the Commission's exercise of implementing powers (European Parliament 2010d)
- Final opinions on draft reports from 12 European Parliament committees
- European Parliament Report on the proposal for a regulation on control by member states on the Commission's exercise of implementing powers (European Parliament 2010e)
- Framework Agreement on relations between the European Parliament and the European Commission (European Parliament and Commission 2010)
- Commission Staff Working Document: Accompanying document to the Communication from the President to the Commission on the framework for Commission expert groups: horizontal rules and public register (C(2010) 7649 final) (Commission 2010a)
- Regulation (EU) No 182/2011 of the European Parliament and of the Council of 16 February 2011 laying down the rules and general principles concerning

mechanisms for control by member states of the Commission's exercise of implementing powers
- Commission proposal for a regulation amending certain regulations relating to the common commercial policy as regards the procedures for the adoption of certain measures (Commission 2011b)

Non-official documents (partly made available on condition of confidentiality):
- Draft opinions and draft reports from 12 European Parliament committees (AGRI, FISH, ENVI, IMCO, INTA, AFET, DEVE, AFCO, REGIO, TRAN, ECON and LIBE)
- Reports on 10 COREPER meetings, Mertens-group meetings and Friends of the Presidency group meetings
- 22 Non-papers, draft compromise texts and meeting documents

Interviews (all interviewees were promised anonymity):
- Four persons involved in COREPER's negotiations and/or coordinating these in the member states
- Five persons working for the European Parliament's committees and services

Notes

1 Hidden Power

1. Figures vary from year to year. See Chapter 2 for a detailed breakdown over time.
2. This mainly includes Decisions pursuant to competition policy and routine Decisions and Regulations on the valuation of imported agricultural products. See Chapter 2 for more details.
3. The Council and the Commission are keen on keeping these expert groups exclusive to member state participation, whereas the European Parliament wants to be able to participate as well. See also Chapter 4, European Commission (2009b), European Parliament and European Commission (2010), European Commission (2010a) and European Parliament (2010a).
4. In a strictly legal sense, after having consulted a comitology committee, the Commission alone decides. Nevertheless, it has to take the committee's opinion into account, such that, in practice, comitology becomes a decision-maker. See also Chapter 2.
5. Both pieces of legislation existed until 1 July 2009, giving quality grades to bananas and cucumbers of different lengths and shapes. They both went through a comitology committee prior to adoption by the Commission (Commission Regulations (EC) 1677/88 and 2257/94).

2 Comitology: The System, the Committees and Their Participants

1. Depending on the voting procedure used, this can be expressed by means of a qualified majority in favour, or the lack of a simple or qualified majority against (see further).
2. Before the alignment of the acquis to the system introduced by the Lisbon Treaty, this was also true for the committees that currently fall under the 'delegated legislation' regime (Council Decision 2006/512/EC). In that regime, the question of whether or not there should be formal votes is settled in the rules of procedure of each and every individual delegated legislation committee (see Chapter 4).
3. Some authors refer to comitology in a broader sense, including all sorts of committee governance, but most follow the legal definition of comitology presented in this paragraph (for volumes in which committees of other types are also discussed, see Pedler and Schäfer, 1996; Van Schendelen, 1998, 2010; Joerges and Vos, 1999; Andenas and Türk, 2000; Christiansen and Kirchner, 2000; Christiansen and Larsson, 2007).
4. With the exception of Van Schendelen (2010) and Héritier et al. (2012).
5. As made available via its digital interface EUR-LEX: http://eur-lex.europa.eu.
6. For a similar overview covering a longer time span, see Figure 1.1 in Chapter 1.

7. This is a conservative estimate. The Commission also adopts executive measures that are not Decisions, Regulations or Directives and are not published in the Official Journal. The share of comitology in the total of executive measures may thus be even greater.
8. This issue is handled by the Standing Committee on the Food Chain and Animal Health, section Animal Health and Animal Welfare.
9. See, for example, http://www.euractiv.com/en/transport/single-sky-wins-support-amid-airline-fears-ets/article-173666, accessed on 12 June 2009.
10. DG stands for Directorate-General.
11. The Ornis committee was added for the year 2005, as the Annex to the Comitology Report of 2005 mistakenly registers this committee as inactive. Respondents (see Chapter 6) also came up with a committee that was not listed: the TEN-Transport Policy Committee. This committee was also added.
12. This issue is the responsibility of the Air Safety Committee.
13. This issue is the responsibility of the Committee for the Deliberate Release into the Environment of Genetically Modified Organisms, and the Standing Committee on the Food Chain and Animal Health, section Genetically Modified Food & Feed and Environmental Risk. The first of these two committees, however, is notorious for not approving Commission proposals, so that in the end most matters have been referred to the Council (European Commission, 2005, 2006, 2007, 2008, 2009a, 2010b).
14. The literature on comitology has placed great emphasis on voting rules. Their roots and their historical developments are covered by, among others, Bradley (1992), Blom-Hansen (2008), Bergström (2005) and Christiansen and Vaccari (2006). For the effect of voting rules on the Commission's behaviour, see, for example, Steunenberg, Koboldt and Schmidtchen (1996), Hofmann and Toeller (1997), Franchino (2000a, b), Brandsma and Blom-Hansen (2010).
15. Council and Parliament Regulation 2011/182/EU uses only two headings for two different procedures, so that only two procedures are said to exist. However, one of these specifies four different possible variants to the procedure, bringing the total to five materially different procedures.
16. Also see Hofmann and Toeller (1997) with respect to strategic use of voting rules under such procedures.
17. Also see Chapter 4; for a historical perspective, see Bradley (2008) and Christiansen and Vaccari (2006).
18. A further comitology procedure known as the 'safeguard procedure' was withdrawn as from the 2011 Regulation. Under this procedure individual participants could refer the matter to the Council. As this procedure has only been applied in two committees, which met only occasionally, it is not mentioned any further.
19. See note 14.
20. This committee consists of six sections for which detailed meeting statistics per section are not available.
21. Seven of these were related to genetically modified organisms, a salient topic on which the member states are notoriously divided (Hofmann and Toeller, 1997).
22. Until the late 1990s it was also common for scientists to join the national delegations to committee meetings (Van der Knaap, 1996; Rhinard, 2002).

There were even several 'scientific committees' that consisted exclusively of academics. However, the BSE scandal in 1996 ended this practice. In order to preserve the independence of scientific advice, the scientific committees were pulled out of the comitology system and their functions were transferred to agencies, agency advisory groups and scientific Commission expert groups (Savino, 2009; Schäfer, 2000).
23. Go to http://ec.europa.eu/transparency/regcomitology/index_en.htm for implementing act committees; http://ec.europa.eu/transparency/regexpert/index.cfm for delegated act expert groups.
24. Article 211 of the EC Treaty indicates that the Commission is responsible for implementation. When the Council insisted for the first time on having a committee set up in the early 1960s, this principle was contested in the Court of Justice. But ever since this so-called Köster case (Case 25/70, *Einfuhr- und Vorratsstelle für Getreide und Futtermittel v. Köster, Berodt & Co.*), implementation conditions like these have been a fact of life for the Commission. The Commission has the power to implement policy, but the Council is free to impose conditions.

4 System-Level Accountability: Conflict Over Control

1. See Agreement between the Commission and the European Parliament on procedures for implementing Council Decision 1999/468/EC, European Parliament and European Commission (2000), L 256/19.
2. Court of First Instance, Case T-188/97.

5 Committee-Level Accountability: System Meets Practice

1. The survey was jointly developed with Jens Blom-Hansen from Aarhus University
2. Rothmans case: Court of First Instance, T-188/97.
3. Rules of Procedure of the European Parliament, Rule 88.
4. Rules of Procedure of the European Parliament, Rule 88.
5. Rules of Procedure of the European Parliament, Rule 103. It is important to note that any parliamentary committee can vote on a 'normal' resolution, as opposed to the RoS and RPS resolutions, which must pass the committee in charge of drawing up the original co-decision act.
6. See http://ec.europa.eu/transparency/regcomitology/index.cfm?CLX=en.

6 Participant-Level Accountability: Substantive Talks and Deafening Silence

1. This is similar to what the literature of representative bureaucracy refers to as 'active representativeness' (Mosher, 1982).
2. Based on the yearly published *Hof & Statskalendern* which is only available in Danish.
3. The committee participants were not asked this question together with the survey to avoid coordination between them and their superiors as much as possible.

4. In a multivariate linear regression analysis, controlled for several other factors, an unstandardized regression coefficient of 0.202 (significant below 0.05) is found where both the independent and dependent variable are five-point scales (Brandsma, 2010b, p. 139). This means that for every full point by which the variable on information increases, scores on the discussion frequency index increase by 0.202.
5. For technical details as to how these dimensions were constructed, see Brandsma (2010b, p. 86–7).
6. Computed as 33.3 per cent of block E, plus 50 per cent of block H, plus all cases in block F.

Bibliography

Documents

Legislative acts, executive acts and court cases

Council Decision (EEC) 1987/373 laying down the procedures for the exercise of implementing powers conferred on the Commission, 13 July 1987.

—— (EC) 1999/468 laying down the procedures for the exercise of implementing powers conferred on the Commission, 28 June 1999.

—— (EC) 2006/512 amending Decision 1999/468/EC laying down the procedures for the exercise of implementing powers conferred on the Commission, 17 July 2006.

Commission Regulation (EC) 1677/88 laying down quality standards for cucumbers, 15 June 1988.

—— (EC) 2257/94 laying down quality standards for bananas, 16 September 1994.

Council Directive (EEC) 92/43 on the conservation of natural habitats and of wild fauna and flora, 21 May 1992.

Council and European Parliament Regulation (EC) 1049/2001 regarding public access to European Parliament, Council and Commission documents, 30 May 2001.

Court of First Instance, Case T-188/97, Judgment (First Chamber, extended composition) – *Rothmans International BV* v *Commission of the European Communities*, 19 July 1999.

European Parliament and Council Regulation (EU) 2010/438 amending Regulation (EC) No. 998/2003 on the animal health requirements applicable to the non-commercial movement of pet animals, 19 May 2010.

—— (EU) 2011/182 laying down the rules and general principles concerning mechanisms for control by Member States of the Commission's exercise of implementing powers, 16 February 2011.

—— (EU) 2011/24 on the application of patients' rights in cross-border healthcare, 9 March 2011.

Other documents from the European institutions

Council (2009a) Report by the Council Presidency to the European Council on preparatory work in view of the entry into force of the Lisbon Treaty, 14928/09, 23 October 2009.

—— (2009b) Report by the Presidency to Coreper on the implementation of Articles 290 and 291 TFEU, 16998/09, 2 December 2009.

—— (2009c) Introductory note by the Presidency to Coreper II on the implementation of Articles 290 and 291 TFEU, 17477/09, 11 December 2009.

—— (2010) Report from the Friends of the Presidency Group to Coreper II, 20 May 2010, 10063/10.

European Commission (2001) Letter from commissioner Bolkestein to Mrs Randzio-Plath, MEP, 2 October 2001.
—— (2002) Report from the Commission on the working of committees during 2001 (COM(2002) 733 def).
—— (2003) Report from the Commission on the working of committees during 2002 (COM(2003) 530 def).
—— (2004) Report from the Commission on the working of committees during 2003 (COM(2004) 860).
—— (2005) Commission Staff Working Document: Annex to the report from the Commission on the working of committees during 2004 (COM(2005) 554 final).
—— (2006) Commission Staff Working Document: Annex to the report from the Commission on the working of committees during 2005 (COM(2006) 446 final).
—— (2007) Commission Staff Working Paper: Annex to the report from the Commission on the working of committees during 2006 (COM(2007) 842).
—— (2008) Commission Staff Working Document accompanying the report from the Commission on the working of committees during 2007 (COM(2008) 844 final).
—— (2009a) Commission Staff Working Document: Presentation of committee activities in 2008 by policy sectors, accompanying the report from the Commission on the working of committees during 2008 (COM(2009) 335 final)
—— (2009b) Communication from the Commission to the European Parliament and the Council on the implementation of Article 290 of the Treaty on the Functioning of the European Union (COM(2009) 673 final).
—— (2010a) Commission Staff Working Document: Accompanying document to the Communication from the President to the Commission on the framework for Commission expert groups: horizontal rules and public register (C(2010) 7649 final).
—— (2010b) Commission Staff Working Document: Presentation of committee activities in 2009 by policy sectors, accompanying document to the report from the Commission on the working of the committees during 2009 (COM(2010) 354 final).
—— (2010c) Commission proposal for a regulation laying down the rules and general principles concerning mechanisms for control by member states of the Commission's exercise of implementing powers (COM(2010) 83).
—— (2010d) Note a l'attention des membres du GRI.
—— (2011a) Commission Staff Working Document: Presentation of committee activities in 2010 by policy sectors, accompanying document to the report from the Commission on the working of the committees during 2010 (COM(2011) 879 final).
—— (2011b) Commission proposal for a regulation amending certain regulations relating to the common commercial policy as regards the procedures for the adoption of certain measures (COM(2011) 82).
—— (2012) Commission Staff Working Document: Presentation of committee activities in 2011 by policy sector, accompanying the document: Report from the Commission on the working of the committees during 2011 (COM(2012) 685 final).

European Parliament (2009a) Resolution of 7 May 2009 on Parliament's new role and responsibilities in implementing the Treaty of Lisbon.
—— (2009b) 'Comitology Handbook: The European Parliament's Work in the Field of Comitology', Conference of Committee Chairs, PE 405.166rev.
—— (2010a) Draft report on the power of legislative delegation, Committee of Legal Affairs, 2 March 2010, PE439.171v02-00.
—— (2010b) Report on the power of legislative delegation, Committee of Legal Affairs, 29 March 2010, A7-0110/2010.
—— (2010c) Minutes of the Committee on Legal Affairs, 2 September 2010.
—— (2010d) Draft report on the proposal for a regulation of the European Parliament and of the Council laying down the rules and general principles concerning mechanisms for control by Member States of the Commission's exercise of implementing powers, 20 May 2010, PE441.207v02-00.
—— (2010e) Report on the proposal for a regulation of the European Parliament and of the Council laying down the rules and general principles concerning mechanisms for control by Member States of the Commission's exercise of implementing powers, 6 December 2010, A7-0355/2010.
European Parliament and European Commission (2000) Agreement between the European Parliament and the Commission on procedures for implementing Council Decision 1999/468/EC, Official Journal 2000 L 256/19.
—— (2008) Agreement between the European Parliament and the Commission on procedures for implementing Council Decision 1999/468/EC laying down the procedures for exercise of implementing powers conferred on the Commission, as amended by Decision 2006/512/EC, Official Journal 2008 C 143/1.
—— (2010) Framework Agreement on relations between the European Parliament and the European Commission, Official Journal 2010 L 304/47.
European Parliament, Council of Ministers and European Commission (2011) Common Understanding, Council doc. Ref. 8640/11 ANNEX, 4 April 2011.

Literature

Abromeit, H. (2007) 'Probleme einer Demokratisierung der Europäischen Union – oder: Warum es so schwer ist, einen gemeinsamen Nenner zu finden', in N. Bandelow and W. Bleek (eds), *Einzelinteressen und kollektives Handeln in modernen Demokratien* (Wiesbaden: Verlag für Sozialwissenschaften).
Agné, H. (2009) 'Irretrievable Powers and Democratic Accountability', in S. Gustavsson, C. Karlsson and T. Persson (eds), *The Illusion of Accountability in the European Union* (Milton Park: Routledge).
Alfé, M., G.J. Brandsma and T. Christiansen (2009) 'The Functioning of Comitology Committees in Practice', in T. Christiansen, J. Oettel and B. Vaccari (eds), *21st Century Comitology: The Role of Implementing Committees in the Enlarged European Union* (Maastricht: EIPA).
Alfé, M. and T. Christiansen (2009) 'Institutional Tensions in the Evolution of the Comitology System', in T. Christiansen, J. Oettel and B. Vaccari (eds), *21st Century Comitology: The Role of Implementing Committees in the Enlarged European Union* (Maastricht: EIPA).
Alfé, M., T. Christiansen and S. Piedrafita (2008) 'Implementing Committees in the Enlarged European Union: Business as Usual for Comitology?' in E. Best,

T. Christiansen and P. Settembri (eds), *The Institutions of the Enlarged European Union: Continuity and Change* (Cheltenham: Edward Elgar).

Andenas, M. and A. Türk (eds) (2000) *Delegated Legislation and the Role of Committees in the EC* (London: Kluwer Law International).

Andeweg, R. (2007) 'A Comment on Auel, Benz, and Maurer', in B. Kohler-Koch and B. Rittberger (eds), *Debating the Democratic Legitimacy of the European Union* (Plymouth: Rowman and Littlefield).

Auel, K. (2007) 'Democratic Accountability and National Parliaments: Redefining the Impact of Parliamentary Scrutiny in EU Affairs', *European Law Journal*, 13(4), 487–504.

Bache, I. and M. Flinders (eds) (2004) *Multi-Level Governance* (Oxford: Oxford University Press).

Ballmann, A., D. Epstein and S. O'Halloran (2002) 'Delegation, Comitology, and the Separation of Powers in the European Union', *International Organization*, 56, 551–74.

Behn, R. (2001) *Rethinking Democratic Accountability* (Washington, DC: Brookings Institution Press).

Bergström, C.F. (2005) *Comitology: Delegation of Powers in the European Union and the Committee System* (Oxford: Oxford University Press).

Bergström, C.F., H. Farrell and A. Héritier (2007) 'Legislate or Delegate? Bargaining over Implementation and Legislative Authority in the EU', *West European Politics*, 30, 338–66.

Beyers, J. and P. Bursens (2006) *Europa is geen Buitenland* (Leuven: Acco).

Beyers, J. and G. Dierickx (1998) 'The Working Groups of the Council of the European Union: Supranational or Intergovernmental Negotiations?' *Journal of Common Market Studies*, 36, 289–317.

Beyers, J. and J. Trondal (2004) 'How Nation States "Hit" Europe: Ambiguity and Representation in the European Union', *West European Politics*, 27, 919–42.

Black, J. (2008) 'Constructing and Contesting Legitimacy and Accountability in Polycentric Regulatory Regimes', *Regulation & Governance*, 2, 137–64.

Blom-Hansen, J. (2007) 'The Danish Comitology Survey. Technical Report', Unpublished Report. Department of Political Science, Aarhus University. Downloadable from the author's home page http://www.ps.au.dk/en

—— (2008) 'The Origins of the EU Comitology System: A Case of Informal Agenda-Setting by the Commission', *Journal of European Public Policy*, 15, 208–26.

—— (2011a) 'The EU Comitology System: Taking Stock before the New Lisbon Regime', *Journal of European Public Policy*, 18, 607–17.

—— (2011b) *The EU Comitology System in Theory and Practice: Keeping an Eye on the Commission?* (Basingstoke: Palgrave Macmillan).

Blom-Hansen, J. and G.J. Brandsma (2009) 'The EU Comitology System: Intergovernmental Bargaining and Deliberative Supranationalism?' *Journal of Common Market Studies*, 47, 719–39.

Borrás, S. and K. Jacobsson (2004) 'The Open Method of Co-ordination and New Governance Patterns in the EU', *Journal of European Public Policy*, 11, 185–208.

Bovens, M. (2007a) 'New Forms of Accountability and EU-Governance', *Comparative European Politics*, 5, 104–20.

—— (2007b) 'Analysing and Assessing Accountability: A Conceptual Framework', *European Law Journal*, 13, 447–68.

—— (2010) 'Two Concepts of Accountability: Accountability as a Virtue and as a Mechanism', *West European Politics*, 33, 946–67.
Bovens, M., D. Curtin and P. 't Hart (2010) 'The Quest for Legitimacy and Accountability in EU Governance', in M. Bovens, D. Curtin and P. 't Hart (eds), *The Real World of EU Accountability* (Oxford: Oxford University Press).
Bovens, M., P. 't Hart and T. Schillemans (2008) 'Does Public Accountability Work? An Assessment Tool', *Public Administration*, 86, 225–42.
Bradley, K. (1992) 'Comitology and the Law: Through a Glass, Darkly', *Common Market Law Review*, 29, 693–721.
—— (1997) 'The European Parliament and Comitology: On the Road to Nowhere?' *European Law Journal*, 3, 230–54.
—— (1998) 'The GMO-Committee on Transgenic Maize: Alien Corn, or the Transgenic Procedural Maze', in M.C.P.M. van Schendelen (ed.), *EU Committees as Influential Policymakers* (Aldershot: Ashgate).
—— (2006) 'Comitology and the Courts: Tales of the Unexpected', in H. Hofmann and A. Türk (eds), *EU Administrative Governance* (Cheltenham: Edward Elgar).
—— (2008) 'Halfway House: The 2006 Comitology Reforms and the European Parliament', *West European Politics*, 31, 837–54.
Brandsma, G.J. (2007) 'Comitologie in de praktijk. Onderzoeksverslag', Utrecht School of Governance, Utrecht University. Available from the author upon request.
—— (2010a) 'Accounting for Input in Comitology Committees: An Uncomfortable Silence', *Journal of European Public Policy*, 17, 487–505.
—— (2010b) 'Backstage Europe: Comitology, Accountability and Democracy in the European Union', Ph.D. Thesis, Utrecht University.
—— (2013) 'Quantitative Research into Accountability', in M. Bovens, R. Goodin and T. Schillemans (eds), *Oxford Handbook of Public Accountability* (Oxford: Oxford University Press).
Brandsma, G.J. and J. Blom-Hansen (2010) 'The EU Comitology System: What Role for the Commission?' *Public Administration*, 88, 496–512.
Brandsma, G.J., D. Curtin and A. Meijer (2008) 'How Transparent are EU "Comitology" Committees in Practice?' *European Law Journal*, 14, 819–38.
Brandsma, G.J. and T. Schillemans (2013) 'The Accountability Cube: Measuring Accountability', *Journal of Public Administration Research and Theory*, forthcoming.
Bundt, J. (2000) 'Strategic Stewards: Managing Accountability, Building Trust', *Journal of Public Administration Research and Theory*, 10, 757–78.
Busuioc, M. (2009) 'Accountability, Control and Independence: The Case of European Agencies', *European Law Journal*, 15(5), 599–615.
Checkel, J. (2005) 'International Institutions and Socialization in Europe: Introduction and Framework', *International Organization*, 59, 801–26.
Christiansen, T. and M. Dobbels (2012) 'Comitology and Delegated Acts after Lisbon: How the European Parliament Lost the Implementation Game', *European Integration Online Papers*, 16: 13.
Christiansen, T. and E. Kirchner (eds) (2000) *Committee Governance in the European Union* (Manchester: Manchester University Press).
Christiansen, T. and T. Larsson (2007) *The Role of Committees in the Policy-Process of the European Union* (Cheltenham: Edward Elgar).
Christiansen, T. and B. Vaccari (2006) 'The 2006 Reform of Comitology: Problem Solved or Conflict Postponed?' *Eipascope*, 2006, 3.

Coen, D. and M. Thatcher (2008) 'Network Governance and Multi-level Delegation: European Networks of Regulatory Agencies', *Journal of Public Policy*, 28, 49–71.

Curtin, D. (2007) 'Holding (Quasi-) Autonomous EU Administrative Actors to Public Account', *European Law Journal*, 13, 523–41.

Curtin, D. and M. Egeberg (2008) 'Tradition and Innovation: Europe's Accumulated Executive Order', *West European Politics*, 31, 639–61.

Curtin, D., P. Mair and Y. Papadopoulos (2010) 'Positioning Accountability in European Governance: An Introduction', *West European Politics*, 33, 929–45.

Daemen, H. and M.P.C.M. van Schendelen (1998) 'The Advisory Committee on Safety, Hygiene and Health Protection at Work', in M.P.C.M. van Schendelen (ed.), *EU Committees as Influential Policymakers* (Aldershot: Ashgate).

Damgaard, E. (2000) 'Conclusion: The Impact of European Integration on Nordic Parliamentary Democracies', in T. Bergman and E. Damgaard (eds), *Delegation and Accountability in European Integration: The Nordic Parliamentary Democracies and the European Union* (London: Frank Cass).

Day, P. and R. Klein (1987) *Accountabilities: Five Public Sectors* (London: Tavistock).

Decker, F. (2002) 'Governance beyond the Nation-State: Reflections on the Democratic Deficit of the European Union', *Journal of European Public Policy*, 9, 256–72.

Dehousse, R. (2003) 'Comitology: Who Watches the Watchmen?' *Journal of European Public Policy*, 10, 798–813.

—— (2008) 'Delegation of Powers in the European Union: The Need for a Multi-Principals Model', *West European Politics*, 31, 789–805.

Delreux, T. (2011) *The EU as an International Environmental Negotiator* (Farnham: Ashgate).

Dunsire, A. (1978) *Control in a Bureaucracy: The Executive Process*, Vol. 2 (Oxford: Martin Robertson).

Eberlein, B. and E. Grande (2005) 'Beyond Delegation: Transnational Regulatory Regimes and the EU Regulatory State', *Journal of European Public Policy*, 12, 89–112.

Egeberg, M. (1999) 'Transcending Intergovernmentalism? Identity and Role Perceptions of National Officials in EU Decision-Making', *Journal of European Public Policy*, 6, 456–74.

Egeberg, M. and J. Trondal (2009) 'National Agencies in the European Administrative Space: Government Driven, Commission Driven or Networked?', *Public Administration*, 87(4), 779–90.

Egeberg, M., G. Schäfer and J. Trondal (2003) 'The Many Faces of EU Committee Governance', *West European Politics*, 26, 19–40.

Eulau, H., J.C. Wahlke, W. Buchanan and L.C. Ferguson (1959) 'The Role of the Representative: Some Empirical Observations on the Theory of Edmund Burke', *The American Political Science Review*, 53, 742–56.

Flinders, M. (2004) 'Distributed Public Governance in the European Union', *Journal of European Public Policy*, 11, 520–44.

Follesdal, A. and S. Hix (2006) 'Why there is a Democratic Deficit in the EU: A Response to Majone and Moravcsik', *Journal of Common Market Studies*, 44, 533–62.

Fouilleux, E., J. de Maillard and A. Smith (2005) 'Technical or Political? The Working Groups of the EU Council of Ministers', *Journal of European Public Policy*, 12, 609–23.

Franchino, F. (2000a) 'The Commission's Executive Discretion, Information and Comitology', *Journal of Theoretical Politics*, 12, 155–81.

—— (2000b) 'Control of the Commission's Executive Functions: Uncertainty, Conflict and Decision Rules', *European Union Politics*, 1, 63–92.

—— (2007) *The Powers of the Union: Delegation in the EU* (Cambridge: Cambridge University Press).

Geuijen, K., P. 't Hart, S. Princen and K. Yesilkagit (2008) *The New Eurocrats* (Amsterdam: Amsterdam University Press).

Gornitzka, A. and U. Sverdrup (2011) 'Access of Experts: Information and EU Decision-making', *West European Politics*, 34, 48–70.

Häge, F. (2008) 'Who Decides in the Council of the European Union?' *Journal of Common Market Studies*, 46, 533–58.

Haibach, G. (2000) 'The History of Comitology', in M. Andenas and A. Türk, *Delegated Legislation and the Role of Committees in the EC* (Den Haag: Kluwer).

Hardacre, A. and M. Damen (2009) 'The European Parliament and Comitology: PRAC in Practice', *Eipascope*, 2009, 13–18.

Hardacre, A. and M. Kaeding (2011) 'Delegated and Implementing Acts: The New Worlds of Comitology – Implications for European and National Public Administrations', *Eipascope*, 2011: 1, 29–32.

Harlow, C. (2002) *Accountability in the European Union* (Oxford: Oxford University Press).

Heisenberg, D. (2005) 'The Institution of "Consensus" in the European Union: Formal versus Informal Decision-Making in the Council', *European Journal of Political Research*, 44, 65–90.

Héritier, A. and C. Moury (2011) 'Contested Delegation: The Impact of Co-decision on Comitology', *West European Politics*, 34, 145–66.

Héritier, A., C. Moury, C. Bischoff and C.F. Bergström (2012) *Changing Rules of Delegation: A Contest for Power in Comitology* (Oxford: Oxford University Press).

Hix, S., A. Noury and G. Roland (2005) 'Power to the Parties: Cohesion and Competition in the European Parliament, 1971–2001', *British Journal of Political Science*, 35, 209–34.

Hofmann, H. (2009) 'Legislation, Delegation and Implementation under the Lisbon Treaty: Typology Meets Reality', *European Law Journal*, 15, 482–505.

Hofmann, H. and A. Toeller (1997) 'Zur Reform der Komitologie: Gen-Mais in der "Filet-Falle"', Working Paper, Hamburg University.

Hofmann, H. and A. Türk (2007) 'The Development of Integrated Administration in the EU and its Consequences', *European Law Journal*, 13, 253–71.

Hofmann, H.C. (2008) 'Mapping the European Administrative Space', *West European Politics*, 31(4), 662–76.

Hooghe, L. (1999) 'Supranational Activists or Intergovernmental Agents? Explaining the Orientations of Senior Commission Officials toward European Integration', *Comparative Political Studies*, 32, 435–63.

—— (2005) 'Several Roads Lead to International Norms, but Few via International Socialization: A Case Study of the European Commission', *International Organization*, 59, 861–98.

Hooghe, L. and G. Marks (2003) 'Unraveling the Central State, but How? Types of Multi-Level Governance', *The American Political Science Review*, 97, 233–43.

Joerges, C. (2004) 'What is Left of the European Economic Constitution?' *EUI Law Working Papers*, 13.

—— (2006) 'Deliberative Political Processes Revisited: What have We Learnt about the Legitimacy of Supranational Decision-Making', *Journal of Common Market Studies*, 44, 779–802.

Joerges, C. and J. Neyer (1997a) 'From Intergovernmental Bargaining to Deliberative Political Processes: The Constitutionalisation of Comitology', *European Law Journal*, 3, 273–99.

—— (1997b) 'Transforming Strategic Interaction into Deliberative Problem-Solving: European Comitology in the Foodstuffs Sector', *Journal of European Public Policy*, 4, 609–25.

Joerges, C. and E. Vos (eds) (1999) *EU Committees: Social Regulation, Law and Politics* (Oxford: Hart Publishing).

Kaeding, M. and A. Hardacre (2010) 'The Execution of Delegated Powers after Lisbon: A Timely Analysis of the Regulatory Procedure with Scrutiny and its Lessons for Delegated Acts', *EUI Working Paper 2010/85*.

Kelemen, D. (2002) 'The Politics of "Eurocratic" Structure and the New European Agencies', *West European Politics*, 25, 93–118.

Keohane, R. and J. Nye (1977) *Power and Interdependence: World Politics in Transition* (Boston, MA: Little Brown).

Kiewit, D. and M. McCubbins (1991) *The Logic of Delegation* (Chicago: University of Chicago Press).

Koppell, J. (2005) 'Pathologies of Accountability: ICANN and the Challenge of "Multiple Accountabilities Disorder"', *Public Administration Review*, 65, 94–107.

Krapohl, S. and K. Zurek (2006) 'The Perils of Committee Governance: Intergovernmental Bargaining during the BSE Scandal in the European Union', *European Integration Online Papers*, 10: 2.

Lane, J.E. (2005) *Public Administration and Public Management: The Principal-Agent Perspective* (London: Routledge).

Larsson, T. (2003a) *Precooking in the European Union – The World of Expert Groups* (Stockholm: ESO).

—— (2003b) 'The Different Roles Played by National Civil Servants in the European Committees', in C. Demmke and C. Engel (eds) *Continuity and Change in the European Integration Process* (Maastricht: EIPA).

Larsson, T. and J. Trondal (2005) 'After Hierarchy? Domestic Executive Governance and the Differentiated Impact of the European Commission and the Council of Ministers', *European Integration Online Papers*, 9: 14.

Lintner, P. and B. Vaccari (2009) 'The European Parliament's Right of Scrutiny under Comitology: A Legal "David" but a Political "Goliath"?' in T. Christiansen, J. Oettel and B. Vaccari (eds), *21st Century Comitology: The Role of Implementing Committees in the Enlarged European Union* (Maastricht: EIPA).

Lupia, A. (2000) 'The EU, the EEA and Domestic Accountability: How Outside Forces Affect Delegation within Member States', in T. Bergman and E. Damgaard (eds), *Delegation and Accountability in European Integration: The Nordic Parliamentary Democracies and the European Union* (London: Frank Cass).

—— (2006) 'Delegation and its Perils', in K. Strøm, W. Müller and T. Bergman (eds), *Delegation and Accountability in Parliamentary Democracies* (Oxford: Oxford University Press).

Lupia, A. and M. McCubbins (2000) 'Representation or Abdication? How Citizens Use Institutions to Help Delegation Succeed', *European Journal of Political Research*, 37, 291–307.

Majone, G. (1998) 'Europe's "Democratic Deficit": The Question of Standards', *European Law Journal*, 4, 5–28.

Marks, G., L. Hooghe and K. Blank (1996) 'European Integration from the 1980s: State-Centric v. Multi-Level Governance', *Journal of Common Market Studies*, 34, 341–78.

Maurer, A. (2007) 'The European Parliament between Policy-Making and Control', in B. Kohler-Koch and B. Rittberger (eds), *Debating the Democratic Legitimacy of the European Union* (Plymouth: Rowman and Littlefield).

McCubbins, M. and T. Schwartz (1984) 'Congressional Oversight Overlooked: Police Patrols versus Fire Alarms', *American Journal of Political Science*, 28, 165–79.

Miller, G. (2005) 'The Political Evolution of Principal-Agent Models', *Annual Review of Political Science*, 8, 203–25.

Moravcsik, A. (1998) *The Choice for Europe* (London: Routledge).

—— (2002) 'In Defence of the "Democratic Deficit": Reassessing Legitimacy in the European Union', *Journal of Common Market Studies*, 40, 603–24.

Mosher, F. (1982) *Democracy and the Public Service* (Oxford: Oxford University Press).

Mulgan, R. (2003) *Holding Power to Account: Accountability in Modern Democracies* (London: Palgrave Macmillan).

Neuhold, C. (2001) 'Much Ado about Nothing? Comitology as a Feature of EU Policy Implementation and its Effects on the Democratic Arena', Working Paper, Institute for Advanced Studies, Vienna.

—— (2008) 'Taming the "Trojan Horse" of Comitology? Accountability Issues of Comitology and the Role of the European Parliament', *European Integration Online Papers*, 12.

Neyer, J. (2000) 'Justifying Comitology: The Promise of Deliberation', in K. Neunreither and A. Wiener (eds), *European Integration after Amsterdam* (Oxford: Oxford University Press).

NRC Handelsblad (2005) 'Een olievlek van ambtenaren', 14 May 2005.

Ogul, M. and B. Rockman (1990) 'Overseeing Oversight: New Departures and Old Problems', *Legislative Studies Quarterly*, 15, 5–24.

Oliver, D. (2009) 'Executive Accountability: A Key Concept', in L. Verhey, P. Kiiver and S. Loeffen (eds), *Political Accountability and European Integration* (Groningen: Europa Law Publishing).

Page, E. (2006) 'The Web of Managerial Accountability: The Impact of Reinventing Government', *Administration and Society*, 38, 166–97.

—— (2010) 'Accountability as a Bureaucratic Minefield: Lessons from a Comparative Study', *West European Politics*, 33, 1010–29.

Page, E. and B. Jenkins (2005) *Policy Bureaucracy: Government with a Cast of Thousands* (Oxford: Oxford University Press).

Palumbo, A. (2010) 'Introduction – Political Accountability Reconsidered: Debates, Institutions, Rationale', in R. Bellamy and A. Palumbo (eds), *Political Accountability* (Farnham: Ashgate).

Papadopoulos, Y. (2010) 'Accountability and Multi-Level Governance: More Accountability, Less Democracy?' *West European Politics*, 33, 1030–49.

Pedler, R. and G. Schäfer (eds) (1996) *Shaping European Law and Policy* (Maastricht: European Centre for Public Affairs).

Peers, S. and M. Costa (2012) 'Accountability for Delegated and Implementing Acts after the Treaty of Lisbon', *European Law Journal*, 18, 427–60.

Peters, J. (2009) 'The Role of National Parliaments: Checks and Balances between the EU and the Member States', in L. Verhey, P. Kiiver and S. Loeffen (eds), *Political Accountability and European Integration* (Groningen: Europa Law Publishing).

Philip, A. (1998) 'The Eco-Label Regulatory Committee', in M.P.C.M. Van Schendelen (ed.), *EU Committees as Influential Policymakers* (Aldershot: Ashgate).

Pollack, M. (2003a) 'Control Mechanism or Deliberative Democracy? Two Images of Comitology', *Comparative Political Studies*, 36, 125–55.

—— (2003b) *The Engines of European Integration: Delegation, Agency, and Agenda Setting in the EU* (Oxford: Oxford University Press).

Pollitt, C. (2003) *The Essential Public Manager* (London: Open University Press/McGraw-Hill).

Przeworski, A., S. Stokes and B. Manin (1999) *Democracy, Accountability, and Representation* (Cambridge: Cambridge University Press).

Puntscher-Riekmann, S. and P. Slominski (2009) 'Comitology and the European Constitutional Treaty', in T. Christiansen, J. Oettel and B. Vaccari (eds), *21st Century Comitology: The Role of Implementing Committees in the Enlarged European Union* (Maastricht: EIPA).

Putnam, R. (1988) 'Diplomacy and Domestic Politics: The Logic of Two-Level Games', *International Relations*, 42, 427–60.

Quaglia, L., F. De Francesco and C. Radaelli (2008) 'Committee Governance and Socialization in the European Union', *Journal of European Public Policy*, 15, 155–66.

Radaelli, C. (1999) 'The Public Policy of the European Union: Whither Politics of Expertise?' *Journal of European Public Policy*, 6, 757–74.

Rhinard, M. (2002) 'The Democratic Legitimacy of the European Union Committee System', *Governance*, 15, 185–210.

Romzek, B. and M. Dubnick (1987) 'Accountability in the Public Sector: Lessons from the Challenger Tragedy', *Public Administration Review*, 47, 227–38.

—— (1998) 'Accountability', in J.M. Shafritz (ed.), *International Encyclopedia of Public Policy and Administration*, Volume 1: A–C (Boulder, CO: Westview Press).

Sannerstedt, A. (2005) 'Negotiations in EU Committees', in O. Elgström and C. Jönsson, *European Union Negotiations: Processes, Networks and Institutions* (London: Routledge).

Savino, M. (2009) 'The Role of Committees in the EU Institutional Balance: Deliberative or Procedural Supranationalism', in T. Christiansen, J. Oettel and B. Vaccari (eds), *21st Century Comitology: The Role of Implementing Committees in the Enlarged European Union* (Maastricht: EIPA).

Schäfer, G. (1996) 'Committees in the EC Policy Process', in R. Pedler and G. Schäfer (eds), *Shaping European Law and Policy* (Maastricht: European Centre for Public Affairs).

—— (2000) 'Linking Member State and European Administrations', in M. Andenas and A. Türk (eds), *Delegated Legislation and the Role of Committees in the EC* (London: Kluwer Law International).

Scharpf, F. (1997) 'Introduction: The Problem-Solving Capacity of Multi-Level Governance', *Journal of European Public Policy*, 4, 520–38.

Scott, C. (2000) 'Accountability in the Regulatory State', *Journal of Law and Society*, 27, 38–60.

Scott, J. and D.M. Trubek (2002) 'Mind the Gap: Law and New Approaches to Governance in the European Union', *European Law Journal*, 8(1), 1–18.
Slaughter, A.M. (2005) 'Disaggregated Sovereignty: Towards the Public Accountability of Global Government Networks', in D. Held and M. Koenig-Archibugi (eds), *Global Governance and Public Accountability* (Malden: Blackwell Publishing).
Steunenberg, B., C. Koboldt and D. Schmidtchen (1996) 'Policymaking, Comitology, and the Balance of Power in the European Union', *International Review of Law and Economics*, 16, 329–44.
Strøm, K. (2000) 'Delegation and Accountability in Parliamentary Democracies', *European Journal for Political Research*, 37, 261–89.
—— (2006) 'Parliamentary Democracy and Delegation', in K. Strøm, W. Müller and T. Bergman (eds), *Delegation and Accountability in Parliamentary Democracies* (Oxford: Oxford University Press).
Strøm, K., W. Müller and T. Bergman (2003) 'Challenges to Parliamentary Democracy', in K. Strøm, W. Müller and T. Bergman (eds), *Delegation and Accountability in Parliamentary Democracies* (Oxford: Oxford University Press).
—— (2006) 'The (Moral) Hazards of Parliamentary Democracy', in D. Braun and F. Gilardi (eds), *Delegation in Contemporary Democracies* (Milton Park: Routledge).
Thompson, D. (1980) 'Moral Responsibility of Public Officials: The Problem of Many Hands', *American Political Science Review*, 74, 905–16.
Toeller, A. (2002) *Komitologie: Theoretische Bedeutung und praktische Funktionsweise von Durchführungsausschüssen der Europäischen Union am Beispiel der Umweltpolitik* (Opladen: Leske + Budrich).
Trondal, J. (2002) 'Beyond the EU Membership–Non-Membership Dichotomy? Supranational Identities among National EU Decision-Makers', *Journal of European Public Policy*, 9, 468–87.
—— (2004) 'Re-socializing Civil Servants: The Transformative Powers of EU Institutions', *Acta Politica*, 39, 4–30.
—— (2009) 'Administrative Fusion: Less than a European "Mega-Administration"', *Journal of European Integration*, 31, 237–60.
Türk, A. (2000) 'The Role of the Court of Justice', in M. Andenas and A. Türk (eds), *Delegated Legislation and the Role of Committees in the EC* (London: Kluwer Law International).
—— (2003) 'Transparency and Comitology', in C. Demmke and C. Engel (eds) *Continuity and Change in the European Integration Process* (Maastricht: EIPA).
Van de Steeg, M. (2009) 'Public Accountability in the European Union: Is the European Parliament Able to Hold the European Council Accountable?' *European Integration Online Papers*, 13.
Van der Knaap, P. (1996) 'Government by Committee: Legal Typology, Quantitative Assessment and Institutional Repercussions of Committees in the European Union', in R. Pedler and G. Schäfer (eds), *Shaping European Law and Policy* (Maastricht: European Centre for Public Affairs).
Van Schendelen, M.C.P.M. (ed.) (1998) *EU Committees as Influential Policy Makers* (Aldershot: Ashgate).
—— (2006) 'The In-Sourced Experts', *Journal of Legislative Studies*, 8, 27–39.
—— (2010) *More Machiavelli in Brussels: The Art of Lobbying the EU* (Amsterdam: Amsterdam University Press).

Van Schendelen, M.C.P.M. and R. Scully (2006) 'Introduction', *Journal of Legislative Studies*, 8, 1–13.
Vaubel, R. (2006) 'Principal-Agent Problems in International Organizations', *The Review of International Organizations*, 2006, 125–38.
Verhey, L. and M. Claes (2008) 'Introduction: Political Accountability in a European Perspective', in L. Verhey, H. Broeksteeg and I. Van den Driessche (eds), *Political Accountability in Europe: Which Way Forward?* (Groningen: Europa Law Publishing).
Vos, E. (1997) 'The Rise of Committees', *European Law Journal*, 3, 210–29.
Waterman, R. and K. Meier (1998) 'Principal-Agent Models: An Expansion?' *Journal of Public Administration Research and Theory*, 8, 173–202.
Weiler, J. (1999) 'Epilogue: "Comitology" as Revolution – Infranationalism, Constitutionalism and Democracy', in C. Joerges and E. Vos (eds), *EU Committees: Social Regulation, Law and Politics* (Oxford: Hart Publishing).
Wessels, W. (1997) 'An Ever Closer Fusion? A Dynamic Macropolitical View on Integration Processes', *Journal of Common Market Studies*, 35, 267–99.
—— (1998) 'Comitology: Fusion in Action. Politico-Administrative Trends in the EU System', *Journal of European Public Policy*, 5, 209–34.

Index

Accountability
  And multi-level governance   11–13, 44–62, 146–50
  As a mechanism   45–7
  As a virtue   45–6
  Checks and balances   48–9, 57–8, 155–61
  Committee level   13, 59, 93–118, 152–3, 157–8
  Cube   139–41
  Definition   45–7
  Failing forums   115–16, 142–3, 162–3
  Fire alarms   52, 71, 112–16, 152
  Multi-level analytical framework   58–60
  Participant level   13, 60, 119–44, 153–5, 158–61
  Popular control   48, 55–7, 150–5
  Redundancy   52
  System level   13, 59, 63–92, 150–2, 155–6
Administrative law   22

Bergström, Carl-Frederik   8, 20, 22, 32, 33, 64–74, 96, 107, 151
Blom-Hansen, Jens   1, 8, 33, 37, 41–2, 65, 95–101, 145, 155, 157, 162
Bovens, Mark   12–13, 45–9, 54–6, 102, 145, 162
Bradley, Kieran   9–10, 38, 42, 58, 60, 65, 68, 70, 74, 95, 114, 145, 147

Comitology
  And delegated acts   6–7, 20–3, 27–38, 72–81, 86–91, 95, 97, 104–11, 117–18, 151–61
  And democratic deficit   9–10
  And implementing acts   7, 21–32, 37, 65, 71, 74–6, 80–97, 105–9, 150–60
  And policy sectors   33–6

1987 Decision   66–9
1999 Decision   69–72
2006 Decision   72–4
2011 Regulation   75–92
Advisory procedure   30
Council referral   64–74
Definition   25–7
Delegated act expert groups   7, 20–1, 27, 31–2, 77–8, 91, 93, 118, 152, 156, 160, 161
European Parliament comitology network   112, 115
Examination procedure   30–2, 82–8
History   63–92
Management procedure   31, 64–74
Non-aligned committees   25–6, 28, 67, 72, 83, 107
Number of committees   25–7
Regulatory procedure   31, 64–72, 106, 156
Regulatory procedure with scrutiny   32, 73–4, 82, 104, 106, 111, 114–18, 151, 159
Regulatory variant to examination procedure   31, 85, 89
Volume of decisions   21–5, 33–6
Commission
  Accommodating behavior   97–101
  Institutional preferences   65–6, 69, 78, 83, 85, 90
Complex interdependence   50–1
Constitutional analysis   57–60
Council of Ministers
  Document forwarding   82
  Institutional preferences   67–70, 77–90
  Sanctions   64–74
Curtin, Deirdre   12, 48–51, 54, 56, 71, 93, 102, 109, 113, 117, 142, 145–6, 152, 156

Index

Delegated acts
  Alignment 32, 81
  Common understanding 81
  Expert groups 7, 20–1, 27, 31–2, 77–8, 91, 93, 118, 152, 156, 160, 161
Deliberative supranationalism 8, 38, 95–100, 120–2, 147, 157, 162

Egeberg, Morten 5, 12, 39, 44, 56, 95–6, 102, 120–4
European Parliament
  Comitology network 112, 115
  Document forwarding 102–4, 108–10
  Information processes 108–13
  Institutional preferences 65–70, 77–90
  Sanctions 104–8, 114–15
Executive decision-making
  Non-controlled decisions 23
  Volume 3–4, 21–4

Failing forums 115–16, 142–3, 162–3
Fire alarms 52, 71, 112–16, 152

Geuijen, Karin 39, 95–6, 121, 124, 134

Implementing acts
  Advisory procedure 30, 81–90
  Appeal committee 21, 30–6, 84–92
  Examination procedure 30–2, 82–8
  Regulatory variant to examination procedure 31, 85, 89
  Voting rules 21, 30–6, 81–92
Intergovernmental bargaining 37–42, 98–100

Joerges, Christian 8–9, 38–9, 95–6, 122–4, 157, 162

Lisbon Treaty 7, 20, 32, 64, 74–92, 105–7, 117, 151

Maastricht Treaty 41, 69–72
Multi-level governance 10–13, 44–62, 125, 145–64

Principal-agent framework 12, 45, 55–60, 163

Rothmans case 71

Schäfer, Günther 8, 10, 39, 46, 66, 69, 95–6, 121, 123–5, 143
Schendelen, Rinus van 2, 5, 8, 22, 25, 38, 41, 95
Slaughter, Anne-Marie 53, 55, 147–8
Style of representation 123–4, 135, 141

Trondal, Jarle 10, 39, 44, 95–6, 120–5, 143
Trusteeship 123–4, 135, 141
Two-level games 12

Printed and bound in the United States of America